WORD
of the
DAY

Merriam-Webster Kids is an imprint of Merriam-Webster Inc., published in collaboration with What on Earth Publishing.

Developed by What on Earth Publishing

Contributors
Cover illustration by Josy Bloggs
Interior illustrations by Josy Bloggs, Emily Cox, James Gibbs, and Liz Kay
A detailed list of illustration credits can be found on p.353.
Text by Patrick Kelly, Renee Kelly, and Sue Macy
Fact Checking by Michael Anderson and René Madonna Ostberg
Proofreading by Nick Whitney
Production Consultation by Marina Asenjo

Staff for this book

Merriam-Webster Inc.: Patty Sullivan, Publisher; Linda Wood, Senior Editor;
Em Vezina, Director of Editorial Operations; Joshua Guenter, Senior Editor (Pronunciations)

What on Earth Publishing: Nancy Feresten, Publisher and Editor-in-Chief;
Max Bisantz, Executive Editor; Andy Forshaw, Art Director; Daisy Symes, Designer

Library of Congress Cataloging-in-Publication Data available upon request

ISBN: 9780877791232
10 9 8 7 6 5 4 3 2

Printed and bound in China

DC/Foshan,China/12/2021

Merriam-Webster's

WORD
of the
DAY

· · · · · · · · · · · · · · · · · ·

366 Elevating Utterances to Stretch Your Cranium and Tickle Your Humerus

uary

JANUARY 1

Razzmatazz
· · · · · · · · · · · ·

(raz-muh-TAZ)

noisy and exciting activity meant
to attract attention (noun)

Circus performers blend athletic skills
with the *razzmatazz* of show business.
Dressed in colorful costumes, they
perform acrobatics and balancing
routines under bright lights as music
blares and fans watch in wonder.

Hoodwink

• • • • • • • • • • • • •

(HOOD-wink)

to trick or deceive (verb)

Frank Abagnale was an American con man in the 1960s who tricked banks, businesses, and people into giving him money and power. At age 16, he *hoodwinked* an airline company into believing he was a pilot by wearing a pilot's uniform and making a phony license.

Proverbial

· · · · · · · · · · ·

(pruh-VER-bee-ul)

of, relating to, or resembling a proverb (adjective)

A proverb is a saying that offers advice or a common truth. The proverb "curiosity killed the cat" suggests that too much curiosity could get a person into trouble. Even without whiskers and a tail, a curious person could be called the *proverbial* cat.

JANUARY 4

Ovation
• • • • • • • • • •

(oh-VAY-shun)

an expression of approval or enthusiasm
made by clapping or cheering (noun)

Born in a small town in the American South,
opera singer Leontyne Price was one of the
most accomplished sopranos of her time. In
1961, she performed the lead role in the opera
Il Trovatore and received a 42-minute standing
ovation—one of the longest in history.

Guffaw

• • • • • • • •

(guh-FAH)

a loud and hearty laugh (noun)

When people laugh, their bodies are producing a strong physical reaction. For a small giggle, the vocal cords vibrate. For a good laugh, like a *guffaw*, air is pushed out of the lungs so fast that the rib and belly muscles spasm. This is often called a "belly laugh."

Epiphany

• • • • • • • • • • • •

(ih-PIF-uh-nee)

a sudden understanding or realization of something in a new or very clear way (noun)

When asked to define an *epiphany*, poet Maya Angelou said, "It's the occurrence when the mind, the body, the heart, and the soul focus together and see an old thing in a new way."

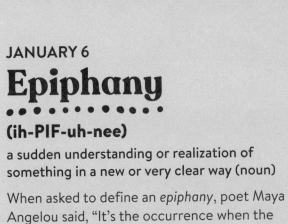

JANUARY 7

Ad-lib
• • • • • • • •
(AD-LIB)

to make up something on the spot without
planning, especially music or spoken words
during a performance (verb)

Many hip-hop artists *ad-lib* to fill in space
between the verses of their songs. Producer
and rapper DJ Khaled's famous ad-lib, "we the
best," was so well loved that he named two of
his albums *We the Best* and *We the Best Forever*.

Klutz
• • • • • •

(KLUTS)

a clumsy person (noun)

In 2020, a *klutz* in an Italian museum
tried to take a selfie and ended up
tripping and falling into a 200-year-
old statue by sculptor Antonio Canova,
snapping off a few of the statue's toes.

Disaster!

When things get extreme,
these words come into play.

JANUARY 10
Fiasco
• • • • • • •
(fee-ASK-oh)

a complete failure (noun)

The 2014 Sochi Winter Olympics
in Russia almost turned into a
fiasco when unseasonably warm
weather melted the snow and
caused snowboarders and ski
jumpers to fall while competing.

JANUARY 9
Mayhem
• • • • • • • • •
(MAY-hem)

a situation with little order or control,
or unnecessary destruction (noun)

A quiet city block in Philadelphia,
Pennsylvania, turned into a scene
of *mayhem* in 2013 when a natural
gas explosion caused a row house
to collapse, damaging two others
in the process.

JANUARY 11
Smithereens
• • • • • • • • •
(smih-thuh-REENZ)

small broken pieces (plural noun)

A stained glass window in Christchurch, New Zealand, was smashed to *smithereens* during a 2010 earthquake. It took 18 months to put the window back together.

JANUARY 12
Pandemonium
• • • • • • • • • • • • • •
(pan-duh-MOH-nee-um)

a wild uproar (noun)

There was *pandemonium* at a 2005 music festival in Glastonbury, England, when heavy rains caused the electricity to go out, tents to flood, and portable toilets to sink into the mud.

JANUARY 13
Hazmat
• • • • • • • • •
(HAZ-mat)

a substance that poses a risk to people's health or to the environment (noun)
Hazmat comes from *hazardous material*.

When an oil spill occurred off the coast of Thailand in 2013, members of Thailand's military wore *hazmat* suits to clean up the black gunk from the country's beaches.

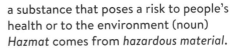

Zany
· · · · · · ·
(ZAY-nee)

very strange and silly (adjective)

Early 20th-century Swiss clown Charles Adrien Wettach, better known as Grock, is often called "The King of Clowns." While most clowns of his era performed outside, Wettach performed his *zany* comedy, musical, and acrobatics routines inside royal concert halls for elite crowds.

Rectify

• • • • • • • • • •

(REK-tuh-fye)

to correct or make right (verb)

When Walt Disney World Resort reopened during the COVID-19 pandemic, all parkgoers were required to wear masks. After a cast member saw a visitor on the Carousel of Progress ride take off their mask, the ride was stopped in its tracks until the visitor *rectified* the situation by putting their mask back on.

Cadre
• • • • • • • •

(KAD-ray)

a group of people working closely
together for a purpose (noun)

In 1943, an international *cadre* of soldiers and
civilians known as "The Monuments Men"
were tasked with protecting historic art
from destruction during World War II. They
shipped important art out of harm's way so it
could be enjoyed for generations to come.

JANUARY 17

Dumbfounded
• • • • • • • • • • • • • • •

(DUM-fown-did)

very shocked or surprised (adjective)

When the New Zealand singer Lorde won two GRAMMY Awards for her song "Royals" in 2014, her mother told a radio station, "As a mum, when I sat there, I was in shock. You feel a bit *dumbfounded* when you hear your daughter's name called out amongst such company."

19

JANUARY 18

Tomfoolery
• • • • • • • • • • • • • • • •

(tahm-FOOL-ree)

playful or foolish behavior (noun)

In her book *Anne of Green Gables*, author Lucy Maud Montgomery had one character describe Anne as "writing stories or practicing dialogues or some such *tomfoolery*, and never thinking once about the time or her duties." That cranky character obviously didn't think writing or acting was serious work!

JANUARY 19

Virtuoso
· · · · · · · · · · ·

(ver-choo-OH-soh)

a person who is an outstanding
performer, especially in music (noun)

Singer-songwriter Prince, born in
1958, was considered a *virtuoso* on
guitar, as well as one of the greatest
musicians of his generation.

JANUARY 20

Quibble
· · · · · · · · · ·

(KWIB-ul)

to argue or complain about
small, unimportant things (verb)

If your friend enjoys a letter you wrote
but complains about your penmanship,
she probably likes to *quibble*!

22

Satchel

• • • • • • • • • •

(SATCH-ul)

a small bag often with a shoulder strap (noun)

Although *satchels* are often used to carry tablets and notebook computers today, they have been around for centuries. In his comedy *As You Like It*, William Shakespeare describes a "schoolboy with his satchel" heading to school.

Where in the World?

Some words come from the names of places that are part of their history. You might be surprised how far some words have traveled.

JANUARY 23
Cheddar
• • • • • • • • •
(CHED-er)

a hard white, yellow, or orange cheese with flavor ranging from mild to sharp (noun)

Cheddar was first made in the village of Cheddar in England.

JANUARY 22
Cantaloupe
• • • • • • • • • •
(KAN-tuh-lohp)

a small melon with rough skin and sweet, orange fruit (noun)

Some of the first *cantaloupes* in Europe grew in Cantalupo, Italy.

JANUARY 24
Denim
• • • • • •
(DEN-im)

sturdy cotton fabric used to make jeans and other clothing (noun)

Denim was first made in Nimes, France. The French phrase "de Nimes" means "from Nimes."

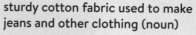

JANUARY 25

Frankfurter
•••••••••

(FRANK-fer-ter)

a cooked, smoked sausage,
also known as a hot dog (noun)

It is commonly believed that
the first *frankfurter* was made
in Frankfurt am Main, Germany.

JANUARY 26

Satin
•••••

(SAT-in)

a fabric that has a smooth,
shiny surface and a dull back (noun)

Traders in the Middle Ages often exported
satin from the port city of Quanzhou,
China. The word used in many languages to
refer to this fabric probably comes from
Zaytūn, the Arabic name for Quanzhou.

JANUARY 27

Tuxedo
•••••••

(tuk-SEE-doh)

a usually black formal suit worn with a
white shirt and a black bow tie (noun)

The *tuxedo* was first worn in the
United States at dinner parties of the
wealthy in Tuxedo Park, New York.

Magnify
● ● ● ● ● ● ● ● ● ●
(MAG-neh-fye)

to make something appear larger
or more important (verb)

Historians believe that British philosopher Roger
Bacon created the first magnifying glass for
scientific purposes in the Middle Ages. This tool
allowed scientists to *magnify* plants, animals,
and bugs to many times their original size.

Provoke
• • • • • • • • • •

(pruh-VOHK)

to cause something to happen or make someone or something angry (verb)

Ever wonder whose fault it is if a dog bites you (other than the dog's, of course)? Well, it depends on the circumstances and where you are. In some places, the dog's owner might be held responsible. But in others, if you *provoke* a dog by yelling at it or taunting it and it bites you, you might be considered at least partly at fault.

JANUARY 30

Hubbub
● ● ● ● ● ● ● ● ● ●

(HUB-ub)

confusion, uproar (noun)

In the 1943 *Looney Tunes* cartoon, "Falling Hare," Bugs Bunny is enjoying a book when he suddenly hears a loud clanging sound. Bugs follows the noise to find a gremlin banging on a piece of metal with a mallet and says, "What's all the *hubbub*, bub?"

Marvel

• • • • • • • •

(MAR-vul)

to feel great surprise,
wonder, or admiration (verb)

In 1939, a company known as Timely
Comics published *Marvel Comics #1*, about
an android called The Human Torch. It
was the beginning of what would become
the fictional Marvel Universe, filled with
superheroes readers and viewers would
marvel at for generations to come.

Story of the month

I had an **epiphany** the other day. My little brother is a **klutz**. I was **dumbfounded** as I watched him attempt a magic trick in front of a **cadre** of friends. There he was, in his **tuxedo** made of **satin**, trying to turn a **cheddar**-wrapped **frankfurter** into a **cantaloupe**. The trick was a **fiasco**. The cantaloupe, hidden in a **satchel** under his jacket, fell onto the floor and was smashed to **smithereens**. I couldn't help but **guffaw**. My poor brother froze onstage like a **proverbial** deer in headlights.

For his next trick, my brother tried to **hoodwink** his friends into thinking he could disappear. I wouldn't **quibble** if the trick had worked, but instead, my brother released a smoke bomb and hid behind an old trunk. Overall, my brother's magic show was far from the performance of a **virtuoso**, and his **tomfoolery** caused quite a **hubbub** in the room. Rather than **ad-lib** a clever excuse, my brother tried to cover up his failures with a lot of **razzmatazz**. He even attempted another trick to **rectify** the situation, but that just ended in more **mayhem**. It was complete **pandemonium**!

Even so, his buddies gave him a standing **ovation** for his **zany** performance. I have to **marvel** at their support, but I worry that their reaction might **magnify** his confidence and **provoke** him to try again. If he does, I might have to show up wearing a **hazmat** suit over my **denim**!

Hear the
story read
aloud.

Febr

uary

Fussbudget

• • • • • • • • • • • •

(FUS-buj-ut)

a person who worries or complains about small things (noun)

Lucy Van Pelt, the leading lady of Charles Schulz's *Peanuts* comic strip, is a *fussbudget* who complains about everything. In one comic strip, Lucy complains that her brother, Linus, makes too much noise. When she finds him making a sandwich, Linus asks, "Am I buttering too loud for you?"

FEBRUARY 2

Yelp

•••••

(YELP)

to make a quick, high-pitched bark or cry (verb)

Dogs *yelp* for any number of reasons. They may be expressing excitement or happy to see the people they love. They may be seeking attention to play or be fed. Or, if they yelp when being touched, they may be expressing pain. In that case, a veterinarian can help distinguish the good yelps from the bad yelps.

Spelunking
• • • • • • • • • • • • • • •
(spih-LUNK-ing)

the hobby or practice of exploring caves (noun)

There are actually two different words to describe cave exploration. Scientific cave explorers call themselves "cavers" and go on "caving" adventures. *Spelunking* usually refers to cave exploration for fun.

Delusion
· · · · · · · · ·

(duh-LOO-zhun)

something that is falsely believed to be true despite evidence to the contrary (noun)

In the Middle Ages, many royals suffered from what is now called "the glass *delusion*." King Charles VI of France believed his entire body was made of glass and even had special clothing made to "protect" his delicate organs.

Woebegone

• • • • • • • • • • • •

(WOH-bih-gahn)

exhibiting great woe, sorrow,
or misery (adjective)

People who are paid to cry at funerals,
called "sobbers" or "paid mourners," have
existed since the dawn of time and can
be found in ancient Egyptian, Roman, and
Chinese texts. In many cultures, paying
people to cry helps *woebegone* families
deal with the pain of losing loved ones.

Grapple

• • • • • • • • •

(GRAP-ul)

to deal with by wrestling,
or as if by wrestling (verb)

The word *grapple* can be used both for physical wrestling and for figurative wrestling, such as with a difficult math problem or other life situation. In the sports of wrestling and mixed martial arts, opponents grapple with one another in hand-to-hand combat, forcing their opponents to the ground.

Punctual
• • • • • • • • • •

(PUNK-chuh-wul)

arriving or doing something at the expected or planned time (adjective)

In the classic animated film *Cinderella*, Cinderella's fairy godmother provides her with a magical carriage, royal footmen, a ball gown, and glass slippers to attend the prince's ball. However, she warns Cinderella to be *punctual*. Cinderella must leave the party before midnight or the magic disappears!

Incorrigible

· · · · · · · · · · · ·

(in-KOR-uh-juh-bul)

not able to be corrected or changed (adjective)

Service dogs train for years and pass a series of tests to ensure they can do work and perform tasks for a person with a disability. *Incorrigible* dogs who fail these tests by chasing squirrels or pulling on the leash are often put up for adoption to be raised as pets.

FEBRUARY 9

Oodles

• • • • • • •

(OO-dulz)

a large amount of something (noun)

In autumn, many small animals including
squirrels gather *oodles* of nuts and seeds
and hide them away underground. When
winter comes, they use their memory and
sense of smell to find the buried meals.
What happens to the seeds they miss? Some
of them sprout into tiny trees in the spring.

Sabotage

• • • • • • • • • • •

(SAB-uh-tahzh)

to secretly and deliberately damage or destroy something (verb)

In wartime, militaries *sabotage* crucial structures such as factories, airports, railroads, and bridges to cripple their enemy's ability to fight. During World War I, British troops cut German undersea telegram lines to stop communication.

Dilapidated

• • • • • • • • • • • • • • •

(duh-LAP-uh-day-tid)

falling apart because of age
or lack of care (adjective)

In the 1800s, the discovery of gold
in California brought thousands of
people to the town of Bodie in hopes
of becoming rich. Today, Bodie is
an abandoned ghost town turned
tourist attraction where visitors can
explore the *dilapidated* buildings and
get a glimpse of the past.

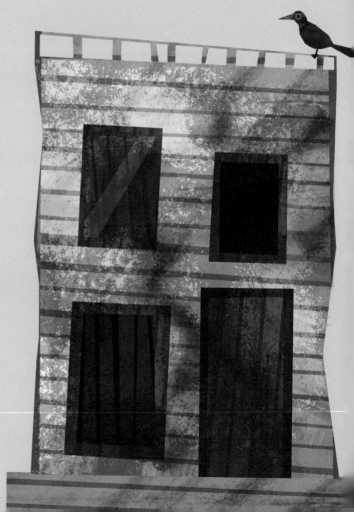

Tandem
• • • • • • • • • •

(TAN-dum)

consisting of things or having parts arranged one behind the other (adjective)

When *tandem* bicycles became popular in the 1890s, they were advertised as "courting bicycles," because couples could pedal together (in tandem) on dates. These bicycles, with one seat behind the other, were popularized in song as "bicycles built for two."

45

Love Language

Love is in the air this month. Do any of these lovely words describe you?

FEBRUARY 13
Ailurophile
• • • • • • • • • •
(eye-LOOR-uh-fyle)

a person who loves cats (noun)

Florence Nightingale, the founder of modern nursing, was also a passionate *ailurophile* who cared for more than 60 cats in her lifetime.

FEBRUARY 14
Bibliophile
• • • • • • • • • •
(BIB-lee-uh-fyle)

a person who loves or collects books (noun)

Ptolemy II was a pharaoh in ancient Egypt and a noted *bibliophile*. He helped establish the Library of Alexandria, which boasted the largest collection of books in the ancient world until it burned to the ground.

FEBRUARY 15
Cinephile
• • • • • • • • • •
(SIN-uh-fyle)

a person who loves movies (noun)

Cinephiles around the world flock to the Melbourne Museum in Australia to view movies on a 105-foot x 75-foot (32-meter x 22-meter) projection screen—one of the biggest in the world.

FEBRUARY 16
Logophile
• • • • • • • • • •
(LAW-guh-fyle)

a person who loves words (noun)

If you weren't a *logophile* when you started this book, we hope you are by the time you're finished!

FEBRUARY 17
Mycophile
• • • • • • • • • •
(MYE-koh-fyle)

a person who loves hunting for or eating mushrooms (noun)

Kennett Square, Pennsylvania is sometimes called the Mushroom Capital of the World. The small town produces half of America's mushrooms and hosts an annual mushroom festival for *mycophiles*.

FEBRUARY 18
Turophile
• • • • • • • • • •
(TOOR-uh-fyle)

a person who loves or is an expert on cheese (noun)

Some *turophiles* turn their passion into a career as a cheesemonger, using their experience and appreciation of their favorite food to sell it to other people.

Aplomb

• • • • • • • • • • •

(uh-PLAHM)

confidence and skill shown, especially
in a difficult situation (noun)

In 2021, *Sports Illustrated* called basketball
player Jimmy Butler one of the top players
in the National Basketball Association (NBA)
thanks to his stellar performance in the
season playoffs. "When the stakes were at
their absolute highest, Butler delivered," the
magazine wrote. "And he did so with *aplomb* . . ."

Wanderlust

(WAHN-der-lust)

a strong desire to travel (noun)

The Travelers' Century Club was founded in 1954 as a social club for world travelers to trade tips, swap stories, and explore new destinations. If your *wanderlust* takes you to over 100 countries, you are eligible for membership in the club.

Mastermind

• • • • • • • • • • • • •

(MASS-ter-mynde)

a person who plans and
organizes something (noun)

In the 1970s and 1980s, rap music
was mostly performed live. Sylvia
Robinson, a singer and record
producer, was the *mastermind* who
decided to record a rap song in a
studio for listeners across the world.
The record, called "Rapper's Delight,"
was released in 1979 and was inducted
into the Grammy Hall of Fame in 2014.

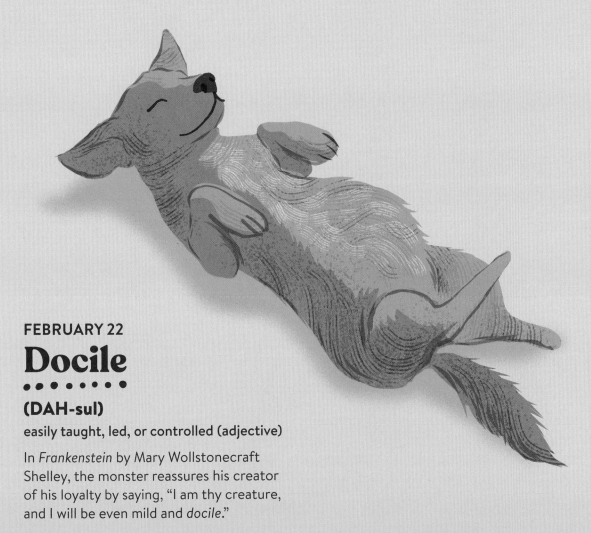

FEBRUARY 22

Docile
· · · · · · · ·

(DAH-sul)

easily taught, led, or controlled (adjective)

In *Frankenstein* by Mary Wollstonecraft Shelley, the monster reassures his creator of his loyalty by saying, "I am thy creature, and I will be even mild and *docile*."

$2a \times 3 = 6a$

$a \times b = ab$

$a \times a = a^2$

$K = P^2/2m$

$a + a = 2a$

$E = mc^2$

$a \div 2 =$

$2a \times 3b =$

$\frac{\Delta E}{\Delta J}$

$Fd\cos\alpha$

$= Ume$

$F_v = \xi \frac{Fn}{R}$

Collaborate

• • • • • • • • • • • • •

(kuh-LAB-uh-rayt)

to work jointly with others (verb)

Famous scientist Albert Einstein and his first wife, Mileva Marić, *collaborated* on his famous equation, $E = mc^2$. Einstein once told a group of friends, "I need my wife. She solves for me all my mathematical problems."

Nag

• • • • •

(NAG)

to annoy by repeated complaining, scolding, or urging (verb)

In 1981, Joan Jett and the Blackhearts recorded a peppy rock 'n' roll song titled "Nag" about someone who *nags* and is "always tellin' me what to do."

FEBRUARY 25

Bailiwick

• • • • • • • • • • • • •

(BAY-lih-wik)

an area in which a person is the expert or has authority (noun)

On *The Great British Baking Show*, each judge has their own *bailiwick*. One judge specializes in bread baking, while another is an expert in pastries.

Glitch

• • • • • • •

(GLICH)

an unexpected and usually minor problem, often with technology (noun)

In 2012, a *glitch* in Apple's map app caused certain buildings and landmarks to seem to disappear. Many users received incorrect directions that led to impossible places, such as the middle of a lake, before the problem was fixed.

FEBRUARY 27

Impromptu
• • • • • • • • • • • • • •
(im-PRAHMP-too)

made or done on the spur of the moment
or without preparation (adjective)

Dr. Martin Luther King Jr.'s famous 1963
speech, "I Have a Dream," ended up being
very different from the speech Dr. King
had originally prepared. He made the
impromptu decision to ditch his speech and
speak about his dreams for the future when
gospel singer Mahalia Jackson shouted,
"Tell them about the dream, Martin!"

Squeamish

• • • • • • • • • • • • •

(SKWEE-mish)

hesitant because of shock or disgust (adjective)

Many future doctors need to get over being *squeamish* about blood. Scientists say gradual exposure can work. For example, it helps to first say the word "blood," then write the word "blood," then look at a picture of blood, and then finally see the real thing.

Quadrennial
• • • • • • • • • • • • •
(kwah-DREN-ee-ul)

occurring every four years (adjective)

The actual time it takes for the Earth to rotate around the sun is 365.2421 days. Most years have 365 days, but every four years we add a day on February 29th to get the calendar back in sync. "Leap days" typically occur every four years in a *quadrennial* pattern. However, centurial years (those marking the beginning of a century, like 1700, 1800, and 1900) that aren't divisible by 400 do not get a leap day.

Story of the month

No one ever said my family isn't adventurous. On our last *impromptu* vacation, we rented a *dilapidated* cabin for a *spelunking* trip in search of mushrooms. My parents are amateur *mycophiles*, but I think they have some *delusion* that they're experts. Still, my mom was the *mastermind* of our trip and handled all obstacles with *aplomb*. She wasn't at all *squeamish* about having to *grapple* with the slime and mud inside the caves. We all did our best to follow her in *tandem*.

I wish my parents didn't have quite so much *wanderlust*. *Quadrennial* vacations would be perfect! I'm a *bibliophile*—and a *logophile*. I have *oodles* of fun reading good books, but I'm a *fussbudget* when it comes to the *glitches* that occur in the great outdoors. I'm *incorrigible* that way. I *yelp* when an insect lands on my arm and *nag* my parents to head home. I am hardly *docile* on these adventures.

It would be great if my parents were *cinephiles* and we could *collaborate* on plans for a relaxing night at the movies. If they were *ailurophiles*, we could stay home with our cats. If only they were *turophiles*, we could eat cheese indoors and avoid the natural elements! But the fact remains that my parents are natural-born adventurers. In the future, I promise not to *sabotage* my parents' plans with my *woebegone* protests. Travel is their *bailiwick* and if they want to explore, I will always be ready for a *punctual* start.

Hear the
story read
aloud.

Ma
• • • • • • • • • • • •

rch
• • • • • • • • • •

Cahoots
• • • • • • • • •
(kuh-HOOTS)

a secret partnership (noun)

In 1950, a group of 11 criminals working in *cahoots* carried out one of the most infamous thefts of all time, robbing the Brinks Building in Boston. At the time, it was the largest robbery in the history of the United States.

MARCH 2
Serendipity
· · · · · · · · · · · · ·
(sair-un-DIP-uh-tee)

luck that takes the form of finding valuable or
pleasant things that are not looked for (noun)

A New York family became millionaires
overnight through pure *serendipity*. While poking
through the items offered at a garage sale, the
family decided to buy a five-inch bowl for three
dollars. It turns out the bowl was made in China's
Northern Song dynasty in the tenth century. The
family later sold the bowl for over $2.2 million.

MARCH 3
Mishmash
● ● ● ● ● ● ● ● ● ● ●
(MISH-mash)
a confusing mixture of things (noun)

Sometimes, the whole is greater than the sum
of its parts. That's the case in Bulgaria, where
a *mishmash* of ingredients makes up one of the
nation's most popular dishes. It includes eggs,
red and green bell peppers, tomatoes, onions,
garlic, parsley, and feta cheese cooked together
in an omelet that is called "mish-mash."

Panache

• • • • • • • • • • •

(puh-NASH)

an elaborate or colorful display of style (noun)

Swedish opera star Jenny Lind was known for both her voice and for her *panache*. In the 1850s, clothing vendors used Lind's name and likeness to sell gloves, bonnets, shawls, and other fashionable garments of the day.

MARCH 5
Liberate
• • • • • • • • • •
(LIB-uh-rayt)

to set free (verb)

In 2010, entertainer Lady Gaga told an interviewer, "I aspire to try to be a teacher to my young fans . . . I want to *liberate* them, I want to free them of their fears and make them feel that they can create their own space in the world."

Hoopla

• • • • • • • • •

(HOO-plah)

great commotion and excitement (noun)

March Madness is a time of great *hoopla* in the world of college basketball. Besides the excitement of the games themselves, the three-week tournament often includes concerts, parades, kids' hoop challenges, and other events in the host cities.

MARCH 7
Madcap
• • • • • • • • •
(MAD-kap)

very foolish, reckless, or wild (adjective)

It's a Mad, Mad, Mad, Mad World is a classic Hollywood film that follows the *madcap* adventures of a group of strangers in pursuit of buried treasure. Constantly trying to outwit each other, the strangers travel across California by car, plane, truck, taxicab, and bicycle, leaving a lot of destruction in their wake.

Avuncular

. . . .

(uh-VUNK-yuh-ler)

kind or friendly like an uncle (adjective)

In the book *Mary Poppins*, Mary's uncle Albert is a jovial fellow who loves when visitors come calling. This *avuncular* man is so cheerful and friendly that he fills up with "laughing gas" and floats into the air.

Words When You Need Them

Sometimes, you just can't think of a word for an object— or maybe you never knew it in the first place. Fortunately, there are plenty of words to use as substitutes.

MARCH 9
Doodad
• • • • • • • •
(DOO-dad)

jabbystick

a small object whose common name is unknown or forgotten (noun)

The *doodad* that looks like a screwdriver with a sharp point at the end is called an awl. Awls are used to make holes in leather, wood, and other tough material.

MARCH 10
Doohickey
• • • • • • • • • •
(DOO-hik-ee)

note bender

an object or device whose name is unknown or forgotten (noun)

The *doohickey* on an electric guitar that rock stars use to pulse or "bend" notes is called a vibrato arm or a whammy bar.

MARCH 11

Gizmo

circle
bulb

(GHIZ-moh)

a usually small mechanical
or electronic device (noun)

A ring light is a *gizmo* that can be used when
taking close-up photographs or making
videos. This circle of light eliminates shadows
and brings out a subject's natural skin tone.

MARCH 12

Thingamajig

wing
point

(THING-uh-muh-jig)

something whose name you have
forgotten or do not know (noun)

The upturned *thingamajig* at the end of an
airplane wing is called a winglet. Winglets
reduce the air currents that push down against
the wing, increasing the plane's fuel efficiency.

Jalopy

• • • • • • • •

(juh-LAH-pee)

an old car that is in poor condition (noun)

"Poppy's *jalopy* is older than dirt," Irish Canadian poet Caroline Pignat writes in her poem, "Poppy's Jalopy." The speaker in the poem lovingly describes the trips she takes with her grandfather in his broken-down car, saying, "It's rusty and dusty, our trusty jalopy. Just perfect for trips made by me and my Poppy."

Devour

• • • • • • • •

(dih-VOWR)

to eat up hungrily (verb)

Cookie Monster is best known for *devouring* cookies on *Sesame Street*, but that's not the only thing he eats. The big blue monster has been known to devour telephones, mailboxes, machines, and anything else that crosses his hungry path.

MARCH 15

Rendezvous

• • • • • • • • • • • • • •

(RAHN-dih-voo)

a meeting that is planned
and sometimes secret (noun)

People aren't the only ones who have
rendezvous. Space vehicles do a set of orbital
maneuvers to have rendezvous with each
other. In some cases, the rendezvous—coming
very close to one another—is followed by a
docking, when the two vehicles make contact.

MARCH 16

Captivating
. . . .
(KAP-tuh-vay-ting)

attractive and interesting in a way
that holds your attention (adjective)

Close to 300,000 people found Bronson,
a five-year-old cat from Michigan,
captivating as they watched his weight-loss
journey online. Bronson weighed 33 pounds
(15 kilograms) which made it difficult for
him to walk. Through a program of diet
and exercise, he lost 15 pounds (6.8
kilograms) and became an Internet
sensation with his own Instagram page.

Concentric

• • • • • • • • • • • • •

(kun-SEN-trik)

having the same center (adjective)

A standard archery target consists of ten evenly spaced, *concentric* circles. The two center circles are yellow, followed by two red rings, two blue rings, two black rings, and two white rings. Archers score points based on where their arrows land and earn ten points when arrows hit the center circle.

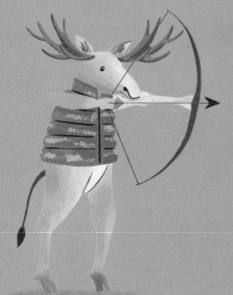

Peruse
• • • • • • • •

(puh-ROOZ)

to look at or read something closely and thoroughly (verb)

The Vatican Secret Archives in Rome were founded by Pope Paul V in the 1600s and are closed to the public. Historians lucky enough to *peruse* the archives have discovered interesting papers from the Roman Catholic Church's history, including a document that offers knighthood to composer Mozart for his contributions to the Church.

Wild Weather

These weather words can make you feel the heat or send a chill up your spine.

MARCH 19
Blustery
• • • • • • •
(BLUSS-tree)

blowing in strong, noisy gusts (adjective)

On April 10, 1996, scientists on Barrow Island in Australia recorded *blustery* winds with speeds of up to 253 miles per hour (407 kilometers per hour) during a tropical storm.

MARCH 20
Balmy
• • • • • •
(BAH-mee)

warm, calm, and pleasant (adjective)

Countries located along Earth's equator have some of the best weather in the world. These tropical regions, including countries like Ecuador, Colombia, and Indonesia, have *balmy* temperatures between 70 and 90 degrees Fahrenheit (21 and 32 degrees Celsius) for most of the year.

MARCH 21
Cold snap
• • • • • • • •
(KOHLD SNAP)

a brief period of very cold weather (noun)

Scientists at a research station in Antarctica observed a temperature of -128.6 degrees Fahrenheit (-89 degrees Celsius) during a brutal *cold snap* in 1983.

MARCH 22
Scorcher
• • • • • • • •
(SKOR-cher)

a very hot day (noun)

Residents of Death Valley, California, are used to hot weather. But one *scorcher* in the summer of 2020 caused temperatures to hit 130 degrees Fahrenheit (54 degrees Celsius).

MARCH 23
Cyclone
• • • • • • • •
(SYE-klohn)

an extremely large, powerful, and destructive storm with very high winds that turn around an area of low pressure (noun)

In 2016, Severe Tropical Cyclone Winston became the strongest ever *cyclone* to hit land in the Southern Hemisphere. Heavy rains and winds spiraled at over 175 miles per hour (281 kilometers per hour) off the coast of Fiji.

MARCH 24
Whiteout
• • • • • • • •
(WYTE-owt)

a type of snowstorm in which clouds and blowing or falling snow make it very difficult to see (noun)

In 2020, one hiker on Mount Rainier in Washington State became lost in a *whiteout* and was stuck in the snow for several hours. The hiker was brought to a hospital where his heart stopped for more than 45 minutes, only to be miraculously brought back to life by doctors.

MARCH 25

Swanky

· · · · · · · · ·

(SWANK-ee)

stylish or fancy, sometimes in
a showy manner (adjective)

Swanky Kong is a rich member of the Kong
family in the *Donkey Kong* video game
franchise. He is a large gorilla known for
giving out coins, bananas, and other prizes
while wearing *swanky* gold suits and jewelry.

MARCH 26

Zigzag
· · · · · · · ·
(ZIG-zag)

to move along a path that has a series of short, sharp turns or angles (verb)

Lightning *zigzags* from the clouds as it reaches down to discharge its built-up electricity by striking the ground.

MARCH 27

Humdinger
• • • • • • • • • • • •
(HUM-DING-er)

a person or thing that is striking or extraordinary (noun)

Serbian tennis player Novak Djokovic played a *humdinger* of a match against Austria's Dominic Thiem in the men's final of the 2020 Australian Open. The Serbian star came back from behind to win the match in just under four hours.

Orderly

• • • • • • • • •

(OR-der-lee)

arranged in some order
or pattern (adjective)

The *orderly* rectangular grid used to
design the streets of Manhattan in New
York City are based on a plan that dates
back to 1811. The numbered crosstown
streets and longer uptown and downtown
avenues still define Manhattan today.

Earworm

(EER-werm)

a song or melody that keeps repeating in your mind (noun)

Some studies have tried to answer the question of why *earworms* get stuck in a person's head. Research shows that they are most likely to occur when a person is engaged in a routine activity, such as cleaning your room or brushing your teeth.

MARCH 30

Motley

• • • • • • • •

(MAHT-lee)

made up of unlike people or things (adjective)

The Bad News Bears is a classic sports comedy film about a group of kids who form a baseball team. This *motley* crew includes misfit boys, a washed-up coach, a talented girl pitcher, and an athletic troublemaker.

MARCH 31

Mojo
• • • • • •
(MOH-joh)

a power that may seem magical and that allows someone to be very effective or successful (noun)

After some early losses in 2018, British soccer player Anthony Martial scored key goals that helped lead his team, Manchester United, to victory. When asked to comment on Martial's talents, British soccer legend Andy Cole said that Martial "has got his confidence back now. He has his *mojo* back . . ."

Story of the month

Last week, on a **blustery** day in the middle of a **cold snap**, my cat Tatiana **liberated** herself from our home and went on a **madcap** adventure through town. It was a **humdinger** of a journey, which I can recap thanks to a **mishmash** of texts from my **avuncular** neighbor, who was able to spot Tatiana from his fourth-floor window despite the **whiteout** conditions.

After taking a few **concentric** laps around our house, Tatiana made her way to a **rendezvous** with her dog friend Scout, who had dug an **orderly** path through the snow from her front door to the street. From there, Tatiana **zigzagged** across the town square, past an old **jalopy**, to **peruse** the **gizmos** on display at the hardware store. Tatiana finds that store **captivating**, even though she has no use for the **doodads**, **doohickeys**, and **thingamajigs** they sell there. I think the owner gives her treats that she quickly **devours**.

Tatiana certainly does things with **panache**. I wouldn't be surprised if she moves to the beat of a fun and peppy **earworm**. The small cat skipped around a **motley** crew of neighbors who were shoveling snow in the town square. I worried that Tatiana might get lost in all the **hoopla**. But it was **serendipity** that just as she was getting tired, our neighbor passed by on his snowplow and gave her a lift home.

As an escape artist, Tatiana certainly hasn't lost her **mojo**. And when she's in **cahoots** with Scout, there's no stopping her. I just hope the next time she decides to visit her **swanky** friend, she chooses a **balmy** summer day or even a **scorcher**. If that cat escapes during another weather emergency, like a **cyclone**, she can find her own way home!

Hear the story read aloud.

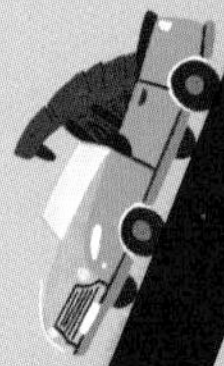

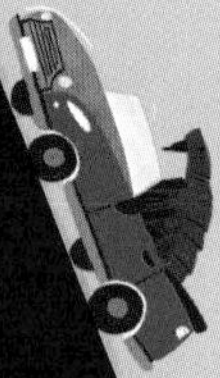

Ap

ril
● ●●● ● ● ● ●

Turbulent
• • • • • • • • • • •

(TER-byuh-lunt)

causing or being in a state of unrest, violence, or disturbance (adjective)

Even very large boats get tossed around by ocean waves. Wind patterns, water temperatures, and underwater earthquakes can all cause *turbulent* seas.

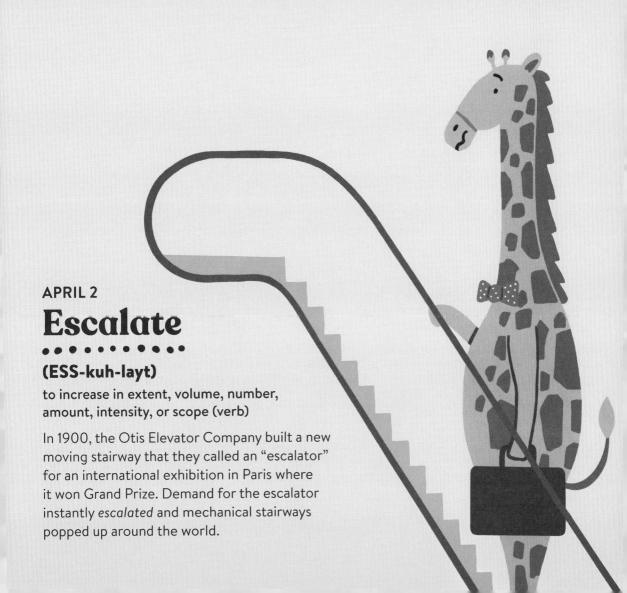

APRIL 2

Escalate
• • • • • • • • • • •
(ESS-kuh-layt)

to increase in extent, volume, number,
amount, intensity, or scope (verb)

In 1900, the Otis Elevator Company built a new
moving stairway that they called an "escalator"
for an international exhibition in Paris where
it won Grand Prize. Demand for the escalator
instantly *escalated* and mechanical stairways
popped up around the world.

APRIL 3

Sputter

• • • • • • • • •

(SPUT-er)

to make explosive popping sounds (verb)

People aren't the only ones who *sputter*.
When an engine sputters, it makes explosive
popping sounds. This could mean that it is
about to run out of gas or that parts in the
fuel or exhaust system are dirty or worn out.

APRIL 4

Egad

• • • • • •

(ih-GAD)

used as a mild oath or an exclamation of surprise (interjection)

A word like *egad* is often called a "minced oath"—a more appropriate version of another expression that is considered unacceptable. In cultures where it's sinful to say the Lord's name in vain, egad is a stand-in for "oh God." Other minced oaths include "gosh" and "holy cow."

Brouhaha

•••••••••••••

(BROO-hah-hah)

great excitement or concern
about something (noun)

In 2000, a bomb-sniffing German
shepherd checking out a New York
museum caused quite a *brouhaha*
when it detected gunpowder. The dog
led its handlers to an empty foot-long
(30 centimeter-long) artillery shell
used in the American Civil War.
It could smell the remains of
135-year-old gunpowder!

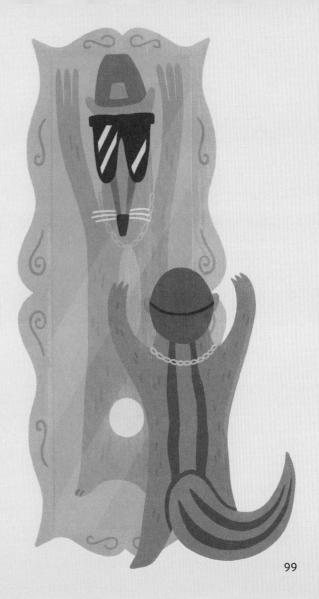

APRIL 6

Ludicrous

· · · · · · · · · · · ·

(LOO-duh-kruss)

ridiculous or foolish; absurd (adjective)

Actor and rapper Christopher Brian
Bridges said he chose the stage name
Ludacris because "my first name is
'Chris' and if you look in the dictionary
under the term *ludicrous* then it means
'crazy, wild, ridiculous'—which pretty
much explains everything about me."

APRIL 7

Colossal
• • • • • • • • •

(kuh-LAH-sul)

extremely large or great (adjective)

The largest known animal to exist on planet Earth is the blue whale. This *colossal* mammal is bigger than any dinosaur ever discovered and can grow to be over 330,000 pounds (149,685 kilograms)—about the size of 30 elephants!

Aghast
● ● ● ● ● ● ● ● ●
(uh-GAST)

struck with terror, surprise, or horror (adjective)

In his 1842 poem, "The Wreck of the Hesperus," Henry Wadsworth Longfellow writes about a maiden caught in an ocean storm and the fisherman who discovers her. Longfellow writes, "At daybreak, on the bleak sea-beach,/ A fisherman stood *aghast*,/ To see the form of a maiden fair,/ Lashed close to a drifting mast."

Flummox

●●●●●●●●●●●

(FLUM-uks)

to confuse (verb)

In her picture book, *The Woman Who Flummoxed the Fairies*, Heather Forest retells a Scottish folktale about a talented baker captured by fairies who demand that she bake them a cake. The baker finds a clever way to *flummox* the fairies and win her freedom while still serving up delicious sweets.

Trickle
● ● ● ● ● ● ● ● ●

(TRIK-ul)

a thin, slow stream of water, people, or things (noun)

Italian astronaut Luca Parmitano was taking a spacewalk in 2013 when he felt a *trickle* of cold water on his head. Before long, his helmet was filling with water. "I experienced what it's like to be a goldfish in a fishbowl," he said after safely returning to his spacecraft. He later learned the water had leaked from his spacesuit's cooling system.

Baby Animals

Come meet these cute and scrawny little words before they grow up.

APRIL 11
Holluschick
• • • • • • • • • •
(HAH-luss-chik)

a young male fur seal (noun)

A *holluschick* spends much of its early life playing with other young seal pups while their parents are away searching for food.

APRIL 12
Cygnet
• • • • • • • •
(SIG-nut)

a young swan (noun)

Although *cygnets* can run and swim a few hours after hatching, they stay with their parents for several months. Cygnets become adults after three or four years.

APRIL 13
Elver
• • • • •
(EL-ver)

a young eel (noun)

Eel eggs hatch into larvae, then become glass eels, then *elvers*. Elvers are about four inches (10 centimeters) long. As adults, some eels can grow up to 11 feet (3.3 meters) long.

APRIL 14
Peachick
• • • • • • • •
(PEA-chik)

the chick of any of three species
of large birds called peafowl (noun)

Adult female peafowl are called peahens and
adult males are called peacocks. Peacocks
display long, multicolored feathers, while
peahens have shorter feathers. The *peachicks*
have all of their feathers when they hatch.

APRIL 15
Spat
• • • •
(SPAT)

a young oyster, clam, mussel, or other
mollusk with a shell that has two
parts connected by a hinge (noun)

Oyster *spats* attach themselves to a
resting spot, where they stay as they
grow into adult oysters. That process
can take two to three years.

APRIL 16
Wiggler
• • • • • • •
(WIG-uh-ler)

the immature stages of a
developing mosquito (noun)

A *wiggler* is sometimes called a wriggler.
Both names refer to the jerky movements
these developing insects make when
swimming on the surface of water.

APRIL 17

Nevertheless

• • • • • • • • • • • • •

(nev-er-thuh-LESS)

even so; however (adverb)

After a female US Senator named Elizabeth
Warren was forced to stop speaking on the
floor of the Senate in 2017, she *nevertheless*
found other ways to make her point heard.
"Nevertheless, she persisted" became a rallying
cry for women fighting against discrimination.

Affable

• • • • • • • • •

(AF-uh-bul)

friendly and easy to talk to (adjective)

Born around 1625, Chief Tamanend, also known as King Tammany, was the Chief of Chiefs of the Lenni-Lenape Nation in present-day Delaware. Tamanend means "the *affable* one" in Lenni-Lenape language, and the chief would talk with other Native American tribes and English settlers to preserve peace and safety for his people.

Salinity

• • • • • • • • • •

(say-LIN-uh-tee)

the amount of dissolved salts in
water or another liquid (noun)

The concentration of salts in a body of
water, or *salinity*, is measured in parts per
million (ppm). Fresh water contains less
than 1,000 ppm. Ocean water contains a
high salinity of about 35,000 ppm, which
gives the water its salty taste and smell.

Kibosh

(KYE-bahsh)

something that serves as a check or stop—usually used in the phrase *put the kibosh on* (noun)

In 2016, the Alaska Department of Transportation put the *kibosh* on pictures of mermaids and fish that had been painted on crosswalks in the village of Haines. While some residents thought the paintings were beautiful, officials said the artwork could cause people to be distracted and lead to accidents.

APRIL 21

Indubitable
• • • • • • • • • • • • •
(in-DOO-buh-tuh-bul)

beyond question or doubt (adjective)

The following facts are *indubitable*:

- April is the fourth month of the year.

- The 21st follows the 20th.

- April is the first month in the year to have a total of 30 days.

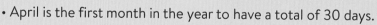

Jolt

• • • • •

(JOHLT)

a sudden feeling of shock, surprise, or disappointment (noun)

In 2018, a man fishing on vacation in North Carolina got a surprise when he went to take a fish off the hook. It turns out he had snared an Atlantic stargazer, one of the few fish able to generate an electric shock. "I felt a *jolt* of electricity go through my hands all the way up my arm," he said. It took about an hour for the sting to go away.

Roundabout

• • • • • • • • • • • • •

(ROUN-dih-bout)

not following a short direct route (adjective)

The shortest distance between two places is not always the quickest way to get from one to the other. *Roundabout* routes such as detours and traffic circles can prevent traffic jams and keep drivers moving even at very busy times.

APRIL 24

Waver
• • • • • • • •

(WAY-ver)

to go back and forth between choices or opinions; to be uncertain about what you think (verb)

English singer-songwriter FKA twigs talked about her experience in the music industry, saying "Sometimes I feel 15; other times I feel fully grown and mature and handling all my business. It can *waver* from day to day, hour to hour."

Words for Nothing

The English language makes much ado about nothing. Here are four examples:

APRIL 25
Bupkes
(BUP-kus)
nothing (noun)

Winning the lottery can be a dream come true, but don't lose your lottery ticket! In 2001, Martyn and Kay Tott won £3 million ($4.25 million) in the UK lottery. Unfortunately, they lost their ticket and ended up receiving *bupkes*.

APRIL 26
Naught
(NAWT)
nothing (pronoun)

Boardmasters Festival is an annual event in Cornwall, UK, that combines live music with surfing and skateboarding competitions. In 2019, festival organizers learned that all their planning was for *naught* when bad weather forced them to cancel the event hours before opening day.

APRIL 27
Diddly-squat
• • • • • • • • • • • • •
(DID-lee-skwaht)

the least amount; nothing at all (noun)

In 1986, reporter Geraldo Rivera hosted a live television special to open a secret vault once owned by notorious crime boss Al Capone. Nearly 30 million viewers tuned in to watch Rivera open the vault only to discover *diddly-squat*—just some dirt and empty bottles.

APRIL 28
Zilch
• • • • • •
(ZILCH)

zero; nothing (noun)

In 2018, two McDonald's customers sued the fast-food company for $5 million for charging the same price for a Quarter Pounder sandwich with or without cheese. The customers thought a Quarter Pounder without cheese should be less expensive. A judge disagreed and dismissed the case, leaving both customers with *zilch*.

Dillydally

• • • • • • • • • • • • • •

(DIL-ee-dal-ee)

to move or act too slowly; to waste time (verb)

Perhaps it's not surprising that there have been at least four racehorses named Don't Dilly Dally. The one who best lived up to the name was a mare from New Zealand who definitely did not *dillydally*. She won four times, came in second twice, and came in third six times.

Swagger
• • • • • • • • • •

(SWAG-er)

a way of walking or behaving that shows bold or brash self-confidence (noun)

In 2008, the American music and entertainment magazine *Vibe* published a "*Swagger*" issue. They explained, "Usually associated with men and the way they walk, swagger has come to mean an overall sense of confidence, style, attitude . . ."

Story of the month

. . . .

There's no **roundabout** way to say this. When I got home from my visit to the aquarium today, I found an **elver** in my pocket. I put my hand in there and with a **jolt**, I felt the slimy thing squirming around. I was **aghast**, as well as **flummoxed**. I had seen lots of baby animals: **wigglers**, **cygnets**, **spats**, **peachicks**, and even a **holluschick**. But I didn't remember any elvers!

Now I know **diddly-squat** about eels and their offspring—**zilch**. **Egad**, what if I killed the little guy? I went online and learned that most elvers live in salty water, so I got out our big soup pot. I started with a **trickle** of water, then more, and added salt, hoping I had the right **salinity**. I was relieved when he started to swim around. Then my mom came home, and you can imagine the **brouhaha**. Before it could **escalate** further, I **sputtered** out an explanation. It sounded **ludicrous**, but it was true!

After that **turbulent** moment, my mom, in her **indubitable** wisdom, put the **kibosh** on my worries and told me to call the aquarium. I **wavered** a bit because I thought I might get into a **colossal** amount of trouble. I was nervous that all my apologies would be for **naught**, and I would have **bupkes** to show for my efforts. **Nevertheless**, my explanation satisfied the **affable** director. She said I should bring back the elver without **dillydallying**. And I did, with a bit of **swagger**. After all, I had managed to keep the little fellow alive!

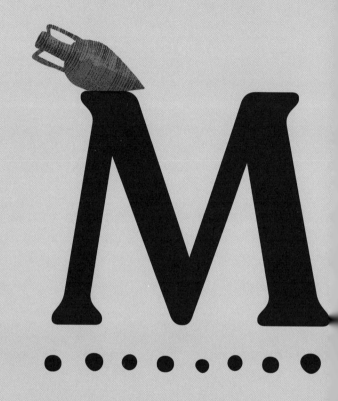

M

● ● ● ● ● ● ● ●

ay

MAY 1
Flibbertigibbet
· · · · · · · · · · · · · · · · · ·
(flib-er-tee-JIB-ut)
a silly flighty person (noun)

During World War II, an American spy named Gertrude Legendre was captured by Nazis. To fool her captors, she played dumb by acting like a *flibbertigibbet* and insisting she was a lowly office worker. The plan worked and she escaped safely to Switzerland.

MAY 2

Antenna
• • • • • • • • • • •

(an-TEN-uh)

a metallic device (such as a rod, wire, or dish) used to transmit or receive radio waves (noun)

The National Aeronautics and Space Administration (NASA) in the United States has a "Deep Space Network" that detects tiny radio signals from space. In order to receive these faraway waves, they use dish *antennas* over 230 feet (70 meters) wide. That's wider than an Olympic-sized soccer field!

123

Oh my! I didn't think I would win. I really don't know what to say. I don't have a speech prepared. I want to thank all the other nominees. You were terrific. I want to thank everyone who helped me get to where I am today. When I was a little kid, I always dreamed I would win an award like this. And I want to tell everyone that dreams do come true. All you have to do is believe. I'd like to thank my parents for their love and support. I'd also like to thank my assistant, my hairdresser, my lawyer, my personal trainer, my dietician, my teachers, my doctors, my friends, my cousins, my grandparents, my godparents, my agent, my manager...

MAY 3

Wordy

• • • • • • •

(WER-dee)

**containing more words
than necessary (adjective)**

In the 1940s, Academy Award winners uttered an average of 113 words in their acceptance speeches. Today, winners give *wordy* speeches that typically clock in at over 250 words.

Verisimilitude

· · · · · · · · · · · · · · · · · · · ·

(vair-uh-suh-MILL-uh-tood)

the quality of seeming real (noun)

Novelist Jane Austen is often considered a master of *verisimilitude* because she created characters that feel like actual people to her readers. To this day, historians continue searching for real people who may have inspired Austen's characters because they seem too real to be fictional.

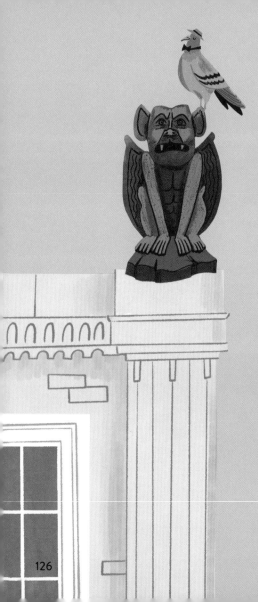

Gargoyle

• • • • • • • • • ••

(GAHR-goyl)

a strange or ugly human or animal figure that sticks out from the roof of a building (such as a church) (noun)

In the 1980s, children submitted designs for a competition to choose *gargoyles* that would sit atop two newly constructed towers on the National Cathedral in Washington, DC. One of the drawings selected was Christopher Rader's idea: Darth Vader. Other winning designs included a man with large teeth and an umbrella, a girl with braces and pigtails, and a raccoon.

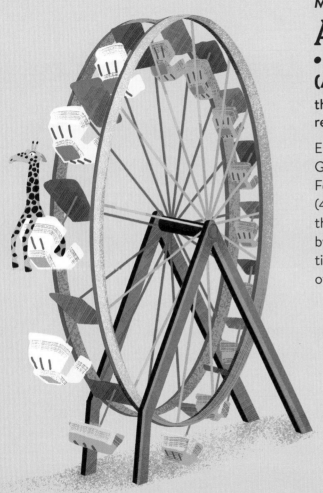

Axle

• • • • • •

(AK-sul)

the rod or shaft a wheel rests on as it spins (noun)

Engineer George Washington Gale Ferris, Jr. created the first Ferris Wheel in 1893. Two 140-foot (42-meter) steel towers supported the giant wheel which was connected by a 45-foot (13-meter) *axle*. At the time, the axle was the largest piece of forged steel ever made.

Raconteur

· · · · · · · · · · · · ·

(ra-kahn-TER)

someone who is good at telling stories (noun)

American poet Amanda Gorman is known as the gifted *raconteur* who recited her poem "The Hill We Climb" at the 2021 United States presidential inauguration. Amanda later revealed that she'd previously struggled with a speech impediment. To overcome it, she rapped along with the musical *Hamilton* to improve her diction.

Retronym

• • • • • • • • • • •

(RET-roh-nim)

a new term used to distinguish the older version of something from the more recent version (noun)

The first bicycles had very large front wheels with very small back wheels. In the late 19th century, "safety bicycles" with equal-sized wheels were invented. Eventually, the first bicycles were given the *retronym* "ordinary bicycles" to tell them apart from the newer, safer bikes.

Digging up the Past

To learn about the past, archeologists go digging for some of these words.

MAY 9
Fossil
● ● ● ● ● ●

(FAH-sul)

a remnant (such as a bone) or trace (such as a footprint) of a living thing from the distant past that is preserved in rock (noun)

In 2010, scientists discovered the *fossil* of a giant penguin in Peru that lived nearly 36 million years ago. The penguin, which was given the nickname "Pedro," had brown and gray feathers and was nearly twice as heavy as the Emperor penguin, the largest species of penguin known today.

MAY 10
Relic
● ● ● ●

(REL-ik)

an object surviving from an earlier time (noun)

In May 2013, ancient mollusk shells were discovered at a construction site in Yuyao, China. These shells are *relics* from early humans who lived in Eastern China approximately 8,000 years ago and ate these oyster-like sea creatures.

MAY 11
Stratum
● ● ● ● ● ● ●

(STRAY-tum)

a layer of rock or soil (noun) (*plural* strata)

Over time, changes in the environment create new layers of soil on the ground. As these layers build up, the weight of the top ones turns the lower ones to stone. A *stratum* of hardened ash may be the remains of a volcanic explosion that happened millions of years ago.

MAY 12
Artifact
• • • • • • •
(AHR-tih-fakt)

an object made by people in the past (noun)

Artifacts discovered in the waters of Lake Titicaca in Bolivia revealed details about the Tiwanaku Empire which lasted from 600 to 1000 AD. Gold medallions, stone carvings, and religious figures dredged from the bottom suggest that the Tiwanaku people made religious pilgrimages to the lake.

MAY 13
Excavate
• • • • • • • •
(EK-skuh-vayt)

to uncover (something) by digging away and removing the earth that covers it (verb)

In 2013, a team of archeologists began to *excavate* fossils in the Rising Star Cave system in South Africa. They have since discovered over 1,550 skeletal fragments from ancient human ancestors.

MAY 14
Coprolite
• • • • • • • •
(KAH-pruh-lyte)

a piece of fossilized dung (noun)

Grass particles discovered in dinosaur *coprolites* near India proved that some dinosaurs ate grass, and that these plants were evolving at around the same time as dinosaurs.

MAY 15

Beneficiary

• • • • • • • • • • • • • •

(ben-uh-FISH-ee-air-ee)

a person, group, or organization that receives money or property when someone dies (noun)

When billionaire Leona Helmsley died in 2007, she left some of her fortune to her nine-year-old dog, Trouble. The small Maltese become the *beneficiary* of $2 million and was hidden from the public to keep him safe from potential robbers.

MAY 16

Uncouth
• • • • • • • • • •
(un-KOOTH)

behaving in a rude way; not polite or socially acceptable (adjective)

Sam Wo Restaurant in San Francisco, California, is known for being a tough place to eat. The most famous waiter there, Edsel Ford Fong, was celebrated for the *uncouth* manner in which he served his customers. He would yell at patrons, sit people with strangers, and constantly forget orders. But it was all in good fun and part of the Sam Wo's experience!

MAY 17

Procrastinator

• • • • • • • • • • • • • • • • • • •

(pruh-KRASS-tuh-nay-ter)

a person who frequently puts
off doing things (noun)

Surprisingly, famed artist and inventor
Leonardo da Vinci was a *procrastinator*.
When asked to complete a project for
a church in Milan, Italy, da Vinci said he
could have it done in six months. The
project took twenty-five years to complete.

MAY 18

Incognito
· · · · · · · · · · ·
(in-kahg-NEE-toh)

with your true identity kept secret, as by
using a different name or a disguise (adverb)

British actor Daniel Radcliffe once
wore a Spider-Man suit in order to walk
around the international comic book
convention, Comic-Con, *incognito*. He
adopted an American accent and even took
photographs with people who were unaware
that it was the movie star in disguise.

MAY 19

Jubilee
• • • • • • • • •

(JOO-buh-lee)

a celebration at the time of
a special anniversary (noun)

A golden *jubilee* refers to a 50th anniversary.
To celebrate Emperor Showa's golden jubilee
as the ruler of Japan, he had a park created to
commemorate the occasion. Showa Memorial
Park in Tokyo spans nearly 400 acres and features
lush lawns, walking trails, fountains, and ponds.

Fuddy-duddy
(FUD-ee-dud-ee)

a person with old-fashioned
ideas and attitudes (noun)

At age 96, American fashion icon Iris Apfel
became the oldest person to have a Barbie
doll made after her. "I never want to be
an old *fuddy-duddy*," Apfel said. "I hold
the self-proclaimed record for being the
World's Oldest Living Teenager."

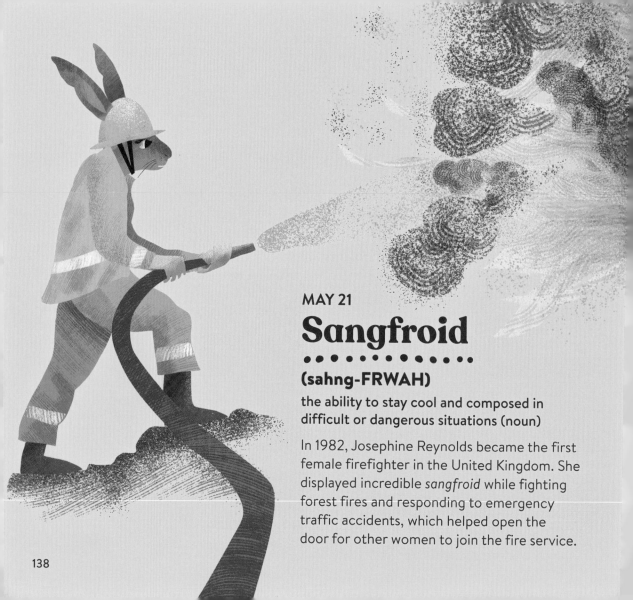

MAY 21

Sangfroid

•••••••••••

(sahng-FRWAH)

the ability to stay cool and composed in
difficult or dangerous situations (noun)

In 1982, Josephine Reynolds became the first
female firefighter in the United Kingdom. She
displayed incredible *sangfroid* while fighting
forest fires and responding to emergency
traffic accidents, which helped open the
door for other women to join the fire service.

Alias

• • • • • • •

(AY-lee-us)

an additional name that someone sometimes uses instead of their given name (noun)

In the DC Comics universe, Superman is an *alias* for the journalist Clark Kent. In one of the most famous comics, Clark darts into a phone booth to secretly transform into Superman to save the day.

Shipwreck

Strap on your life jacket and get ready to take a plunge! When ships sink, these words float to the top.

MAY 23
Castaway
• • • • • • • •
(KAST-uh-way)

a person who has been left alone in an isolated place as a result of a storm, shipwreck, etc. (noun)

In 1857, a ship, the *Saint-Paul*, hit a reef off the coast of New Guinea and was wrecked. A cabin boy named Narcisse Pelletier and some others survived, traveling by longboat over 600 miles (965 kilometers) to Australia, where Narcisse was abandoned and became a *castaway*. He was eventually rescued by local Aboriginal people and lived with them for the next 17 years before being spotted by a British ship and taken back to France.

MAY 24
Jetsam
• • • • • • • •
(JET-sum)

floating objects that are thrown overboard from a ship to lighten the ship's load (noun)

In 1782, a British ship destined for America got stuck in a sandbar off the coast of Florida. While all the passengers made it off safely, historians believe that the crew tossed a heavy lead pump, cannons, and other *jetsam* overboard in an attempt to lighten the ship's load and free it from the sand.

MAY 25
Salvage
• • • • • • • •
(SAL-vij)

to rescue or save from wreckage or ruin (verb)

In the 1780s, the British ship *Hartwell* sank along the coast of Cape Verde in Western Africa. In the 1990s, a South African company sent researchers to the bottom of the ocean to *salvage* silver coins and other artifacts from the wreck.

MAY 26
Flotsam
• • • • • • • •

(FLAHT-sum)

floating wreckage of a ship or its cargo (noun)

In 1997, nearly five million Lego bricks fell into the ocean during a shipping voyage. This colorful *flotsam* traveled on ocean currents all around the world with Lego bricks washing up on beaches from Europe to Australia.

MAY 27
Capsize
• • • • • • •

(KAP-syze)

to turn upside down in the water (verb)

On September 8, 2019, a Korean ship called the *MV Golden Ray* took on water and *capsized* off the coast of the United States. Luckily, the crew escaped the 656-foot-long (200-meter-long) ship, and everyone was safely rescued.

Contend

• • • • • • • • •

(kun-TEND)

to struggle to overcome something (verb)

"Stagecoach Mary" was the nickname given to Mary Fields, the first African American woman to become a Star Route Carrier for the US Post Office in 1895. She delivered mail in a horse-drawn stagecoach and had to *contend* with dangers like wolves, brutal weather conditions, and even robbers. Despite these dangers, she never missed a day of work in eight years.

MAY 29

Skyrocket
· · · · · · · · · · · · ·
(SKYE-rah-kut)

to shoot up suddenly (verb)

To create a soda rocket (and a big mess!) all you need is a bottle of diet cola and a pack of Mentos mints. When you drop Mentos into a bottle of diet cola, carbon dioxide molecules from the soda attach to the mints and create giant bubbles, causing fizzy soda to *skyrocket* into the air. Don't attempt this trick unless you plan to get wet!

MAY 30
Scoundrel
• • • • • • • • • • •
(SKOWN-drul)

a person who is cruel or dishonest (noun)

Charles Ponzi was an Italian American con man who posed as a financial master in 1920 and promised people large sums of money on investments. The only issue though was that there were no real investments. Ponzi was simply moving money from new investors to pay off old investors, while taking money from everyone in the process. By the time he was caught, the *scoundrel* had stolen $15 million.

MAY 31

Defenestrate
· · · · · · · · · · · · ·

(dee-FEN-uh-strayt)

to throw a person or thing
out of a window (verb)

Comedian Mike Birbiglia suffers from a rare
sleep disorder that leads to sleepwalking.
Once, when he was staying at a hotel, he
had a sleepwalking episode so extreme
that it caused him to *defenestrate* himself.
Though frightening in the moment, it
made for big laughs on stage.

Story of the month

Every Friday night, Jacelle and her friends play the adventure-fantasy role-playing game, *The Realm of Imperium*. This week's game is a *jubilee* because the group has been playing for one year. Jacelle and her friends love going *incognito* as their game *aliases*. Kamal plays a *scoundrel* wizard only looking for his pay day. Daniel plays an *uncouth* troll with a chip on his shoulder. Teddy dives into the role of a *gargoyle* capable of flight and strength. Rosa becomes an archer with great aim and an abundance of *sangfroid*. And Sydney becomes a *fuddy-duddy* robot who only plays classical music and controls sound through her *antenna*.

Jacelle plays the role of the game-master. At school, Jacelle gets anxious and sometimes feels like a *wordy flibbertigibbet*. But when she leads the game, she becomes a gifted *raconteur* capable of a *verisimilitude* that brings the game to life.

"This week," she says, "the realm must *contend* with evil forces while returning stolen *relics* and *artifacts* to their rightful tombs across sea." Kamal starts the game by trading a magic potion to become a sea captain's *beneficiary*, gaining access to the captain's ship. The players climb onboard to start their voyage as disaster strikes. "Oh no!" Janelle shouts. "A sea dragon hit the ship and sent everything *skyrocketing*!" As the ship *capsizes*, the players *defenestrate* themselves through the portholes. Kamal, Daniel, Teddy, and Sydney cling to *flotsam* and *jetsam* in the water while Rosa dives to the ocean floor to *salvage* the relics and artifacts that toppled overboard. The *castaways* then swim to a nearby island to continue their mission.

When they reach land, Teddy—who is usually a **procrastinator**—is the first to discover the tomb. The players turn a wheel that turns an **axle** to open the tomb's door. Once inside, Daniel **excavates strata** and removes **fossils** and **coprolites** from the dirt until he uncovers a golden box. Finally, the players place the relics and artifacts in the box to win the game. "Great job!" Jacelle tells her friends, "But an expansion pack called *The Realm of New Imperium* comes out next week. The game we've been playing now goes by the **retronym**, *The Realm of Old Imperium*. See you again next Friday!"

Hear the story read aloud.

Ju

ne
● ● ● ● ● ●

JUNE 1

Befuddle

• • • • • • • • • •

(bih-FUD-ul)

to make (someone) unable
to think clearly (verb)

When asked about his research in a
2007 interview, astrophysicist Neil
deGrasse Tyson said, "If a scientist is not
befuddled by what they're looking at,
then they're not a research scientist."

JUNE 2

Impetus
• • • • • • • • • •
(IM-puh-tus)

a force that causes something (such as a process or activity) to be done (noun)

Ever want to write an invisible message? Squeeze lemon juice into a glass, add a few drops of water, and mix it together. Then, dip a paintbrush into the mixture and write a message on some paper. After it dries, heat the paper with a hair dryer and the message will reappear! Lemon juice contains acid that only darkens when heated, so the hot air acts as the *impetus* for your secret message to be revealed.

151

Kerfuffle
• • • • • • • • • •

(ker-FUFF-ul)

a disturbance or commotion typically caused by a dispute or conflict (noun)

In 1849, the Astor Place Riot in New York City resulted in hundreds of injuries and the deaths of at least 22 people. The *kerfuffle* occurred due to the professional rivalry between American actor Edwin Forrest and British actor William Macready. While Macready performed Macbeth at the Astor Place Opera House, a crowd of more than 10,000 people, mostly fans of Forrest, attacked the theater and a violent clash ensued.

JUNE 4

Bamboozle
• • • • • • • • • • • • •
(bam-BOO-zul)

to trick or confuse (verb)

Anansi the Spider is a character
from West African folklore known
to *bamboozle* people to get what he
wants. In one story, Anansi tricks
the Sky God, Nyame, into selling
him all the stories in the universe.

153

JUNE 5

Domesticate
· · · · · · · · · · · · · · · · ·

(duh-MESS-tih-kayt)

to breed or train an animal to need and accept the care of human beings (verb)

Thousands of years ago, wild chickens weighed about two pounds and laid a small number of eggs. Humans *domesticated* the animal over time and bred it to be larger to provide more meat. Now, domestic chickens typically weigh up to 17 pounds (3 kilograms) and often produce 200 or more eggs a year.

JUNE 6
Exasperate
. . . .
(ig-ZASS-puh-rayt)

to make (someone) very
angry or annoyed (verb)

In 2014, psychologists studied why
"rage quitting" is common among
video game players. They found that
playing poorly and being beaten by
another player, or even a computer,
exasperates them. This threatens
their ego and causes an outburst.

155

JUNE 7

Ruse

• • • • • •

(ROOZ)

**an action intended to deceive
or trick someone (noun)**

Aesop's Fables tell the story of a wolf who
wears sheepskin as a *ruse* to blend in with
the flock and eat the sheep at nightfall.
Unfortunately, a hungry shepherd ruins
the wolf's plan when he goes to kill a
sheep for dinner . . . and chooses the wolf!

Omnibus

• • • • • • • • • • •

(AHM-nih-bus)

a book containing reprints of a number
of works (as of a single author or on
a single subject) (noun)

Writer J. R. R. Tolkien's famous novel, *The
Lord of the Rings*, is comprised of three
books: *The Fellowship of the Ring*, *The Two
Towers*, and *The Return of the King*. The novel
is sold as an *omnibus* containing all three
books plus six appendices, bringing the
total word count to around half a million!

Pachyderm

• • • • • • • • • • • • •

(PAK-ih-derm)

a type of animal that has
hooves and thick skin (noun)

The rhinoceros is a type of *pachyderm*,
and so are hippos and elephants.
There are five different species of
rhinos—two found in Africa (black and
white rhinos) and three in Asia (Indian,
Sumatran, and Javan rhinos). Rhinos
love mud and are often seen rolling
around in it to give them a "mud coat"
which helps keep them cool and stops
insects from biting.

Septillion

· · · · · · · · · ◆

(sep-TIL-yun)

a number equal to 1 followed by 24 zeros
(1,000,000,000,000,000,000,000,000) (noun)

Each year during winter, the earth receives a *septillion*
snowflakes. That's a trillion trillion snow crystals!

Rubberneck

(RUB-er-nek)

to look around or stare with great curiosity; to slow down while you are driving in order to stare at something (verb)

In 2017, the company SpaceX launched a rocket in order to send satellites into space. The launch was a success, but all the people *rubbernecking* on the freeway below caused a multicar crash.

Doppelganger

(DAH-pul-gang-er)

a ghostly counterpart or lookalike of a living person (noun)

Edgar Allen Poe's horror tale *William Wilson* tells the story of a boy who meets his *doppelganger*. Throughout William's life, his double works tirelessly to ruin his plans until William finally kills him. Unfortunately, the double was only in William's head and he accidentally ends his own life.

Robotic Words

Check out these mechanical words and get ready for the robot revolution!

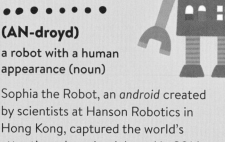

JUNE 13
Cyborg
● ● ● ● ● ● ●

(SYE-borg)

a creature that is part human and part machine or a person whose body contains mechanical or electrical devices that provide more power than the average human (noun)

Spanish artist Neil Harbisson was diagnosed with complete color blindness as a child. Working with computer scientists, he had a sensor and antenna implanted into his brain that translates colors into sound waves. Now, Harbisson can detect ultraviolet and infrared colors invisible to the human eye in addition to colors other humans can see. Harbisson considers himself to be the first *cyborg* legally recognized by a government.

JUNE 14
Android
● ● ● ● ● ● ●

(AN-droyd)

a robot with a human appearance (noun)

Sophia the Robot, an *android* created by scientists at Hanson Robotics in Hong Kong, captured the world's attention when she debuted in 2016. Sophia looks and talks like a human and can even recognize people's facial expressions and tone of voice.

JUNE 15
Debug
● ● ● ● ● ● ●

(dee-BUG)

to identify and remove errors from computer hardware or software (verb)

In February 2013, scientists lost communication with the Mars rover, *Curiosity*, due to a mechanical issue. Team members *debugged* the rover from over 175 million miles (281 million kilometers) away and were able to recover communication three weeks later.

JUNE 16
Automation
• • • • • • • • • •

(aw-tuh-MAY-shun)

the process of replacing human labor with a system of mechanical or electronic operations (noun)

As robotics improve, more jobs are being replaced by machines. The accounting firm PricewaterhouseCoopers (PwC) predicts that by 2030, nearly 30 percent of all jobs may be eliminated due to *automation*.

JUNE 17
Actuator
• • • • • • • • •

(AK-chuh-way-ter)

the part of a machine that makes something move or operate (noun)

When you walk into a grocery store and the doors automatically open, an *actuator* is providing the energy to make the doors move.

JUNE 18
Prototype
• • • • • • • • • •

(PROH-tuh-type)

an original or first model of something from which other forms are copied or developed (noun)

In 2015, Google unveiled the *prototype* for a self-driving car. Unfortunately, the car was involved in 11 minor traffic accidents and further testing was needed.

163

Troubadour

• • • • • • • • • • • •

(TROO-buh-dor)

a singer, especially of folk songs (noun)

Woody Guthrie was an influential American folk singer whose songs focused on the struggles of common people, especially during the Great Depression. The *troubadour* is perhaps most famous for his song, "This Land Is Your Land," which was especially popular during the civil rights movement of the 1960s.

Abhor
· · · · · · · ·

(ub-HOR)

to dislike someone or something very much (verb)

Cilantro is a leaf similar to basil or parsley that is often used in cooking. But some people *abhor* it. That's because they have a gene that makes this popular herb taste like soap!

Recumbent

• • • • • • • • • • • • •

(rih-KUM-bunt)

lying down (adjective)

In the 1930s, French bicycle builder Charles Mochet shocked the world with a new kind of bicycle when its rider traveled over 28 miles per hour (45 kilometers per hour) and set a new world record. Low to the ground, the design of his bike had riders in a *recumbent* position, almost lying on their backs rather than sitting upright. It caused such outrage that the International Cyclist's Union came out with a new definition of a racing bicycle that essentially banned recumbent bikes.

JUNE 22

Ecosystem
• • • • • • • • • • • • • •

(EE-koh-siss-tum)

an interconnected community of living
things that interact with one another
and their environment (noun)

The Amazon Rainforest in South America
is perhaps the world's most diverse
ecosystem. Currently, about 390 billion
trees and 10 percent of all animal species
on Earth call the Amazon Rainforest home.

Squeegee

• • • • • • • • • • •

(SKWEE-jee)

a tool made out of a blade of rubber attached to a handle that is used for spreading or wiping liquid on, across, or off a surface (noun)

Each year, the International Window Cleaning Association hosts a convention with an official speed-cleaning contest. Each contestant uses a *squeegee* to wipe windows clean until there are no visible streaks or smears. Judged by an expert referee, each smear detected gets a half-second penalty.

JUNE 24

Harbinger

• • • • • • • • • • •

(HAHR-bun-jer)

a person or thing that announces the arrival of another person or thing (noun)

There is a belief in the British Isles and parts of Europe that chimney sweeps are *harbingers* of good luck. Newlywed couples often hire chimney sweeps to greet them on their wedding day to ensure good luck for the future.

Curlicue
• • • • • • • • • •

(KER-lee-kyoo)

a decoratively curved line or shape (noun)

In cartoons, pigs are usually portrayed as plump pink animals with corkscrew-shaped tails. But not all species of pigs have *curlicues* on their rear ends. Most wild pigs actually have straight tails.

JUNE 26

Ponder

• • • • • • •

(PAHN-der)

to think about or consider
(something) carefully (verb)

Henry David Thoreau was an American
writer who, in 1845, moved to the
woods near Concord, Massachusetts.
For over two years, he lived in a cabin
he built himself near Walden Pond.
Thoreau wanted to escape civilization,
and he used this time to *ponder* his
life, his writing, and society. His
experiences culminated in his famous
book, *Walden; or, Life in the Woods*.

171

Turbine

• • • • • • • • •

(TUR-bun)

a spinning engine that turns the movement of water, steam, gas, air, or another fluid into energy (noun)

Windmills located in the town of Nashtifan, Iran, are some of the oldest in the world. Made from clay, straw, and wood, the *turbines* can withstand winds of up to 74 miles per hour (110 kilometers per hour).

Demolish

• • • • • • • • • •

(dih-MAH-lish)

to destroy, tear down, or take apart (verb)

The original Pennsylvania Station, a train station in New York City, opened in 1910 and stretched eight acres. The waiting room was inspired by a famous Roman bath with 148 foot (45 meter) high ceilings. However, by the 1960s the building had fallen into decline and was *demolished*. In response to public uproar, the city created the Landmarks Preservation Commission, which has since saved almost 1,500 landmarks from destruction.

Honorary

• • • • • • • • • • • •

(AH-nuh-rair-ee)

given or elected in recognition of
achievement or service without the
usual requirements (adjective)

In 1981, a black dog named Bosco beat
two people in an election and was named
honorary mayor of Sunol, California. Though
the current mayor is a human, a bronze
statue of the friendly dog now stands
permanently at the town's post office.

Pompadour

• • • • • • • • • • • • •

(PAHM-puh-dor)

a style of hairdressing in which the hair is combed into a high mound in front (noun)

In Japan, members of the modern-day subculture group the Tokyo Rockabilly Club sport gravity-defying *pompadours* and dance in Yoyogi Park to celebrate the era of 1950's American rock 'n' roll.

Story of the month

· ·

Lucy always wanted to be a comic book writer. The *impetus* for this career path was the old *omnibus* sci-fi comic book, *Orion Colt: Space Troubadour*, which she read as a kid. The series follows Orion Colt, a star-traveling, folk-singing *cyborg* with a *curlicue pompadour* and a state-of-the-art *prototype* laser guitar. His sidekick is QE-5, an *exasperated android* with a built-in *squeegee*. The folk-singing robots battle Overlord Dorn, an evil force who emits a foul smell as a *harbinger* of impending doom. Dorn seeks to destroy the *ecosystem* of every planet so he can control more than one *septillion* living organisms for himself.

In Lucy's favorite adventure, Orion holds a concert and gets Overlord Dorn to attend. Riding atop a *domesticated pachyderm*, Dorn moves through the *rubbernecking* crowd to get closer to Orion. But when he reaches the stage, Dorn realizes that the singer is not Orion, but his *doppelganger*! The concert was merely a *ruse* for Orion to sneak onto Dorn's ship. As Dorn rages, Orion *debugs* the ship's *automation* using his built-in *actuator*. He hits a shiny red button and *demolishes* the engine's *turbines*, destroying Dorn's only means of transportation!

As a young girl, Lucy would lie *recumbent* for hours *pondering* the Orion Colt series. Years later, she created her own comic book series about a time-traveling punk band, Abby and the Wildcats. But as Lucy's writing career blossomed, she heard about a *kerfuffle* between Gary Cohen, the creator of Orion Colt, and his manager. Sadly, Gary Cohen's manager *bamboozled* the writer out of all his money!

Lucy was ***befuddled*** by what to do next, but she ***abhorred*** the situation and had to help. Eventually, Lucy recommended Gary to receive a Lifetime Achievement Award for his contribution to comic books. Gary won the award and received a large cash prize. To thank Lucy for her help, he listed her as an ***honorary*** co-writer for his newest Orion Colt comic.

Hear the story read aloud.

Ju

..ly

JULY 1

Ephemeral

· · · · · · · · · · · · ·

(ih-FEM-uh-rul)

lasting a very short time (adjective)

The Queen of the Night is a flowering cactus whose flowers grow from small stems to over one foot long and only bloom for a single night. The *ephemeral* flowers open at dusk and begin to wilt as soon as the sun hits them the following morning.

Intransigent

(in-TRANSS-uh-junt)

refusing to compromise or abandon an
extreme position or attitude (adjective)

Joseph Bazalgette was the chief engineer of
the London sewer network in the mid-1800s.
Original plans called for narrow tunnels, but
the *intransigent* Bazalgette demanded
that the tunnels be enlarged to
double their size in case of
unforeseen circumstances.
Thanks to his thinking, the
sewer system was able to
handle an unexpected
population growth a
hundred years later.
The brick-lined
tunnels are still
used today.

181

Lavation

• • • • • • • • • • •

(lay-VAY-shuhn)

the act of washing or cleansing (noun)

In 2017, a company in Katy, Texas entered the world-record books as the longest car wash in the world. Vehicles move through numerous water sprayers and suds, 25 foam brushes, and 17 blowers during the 255-foot-long (77-meter-long) *lavation*.

JULY 4

Bugaboo
• • • • • • • • • • •

(BUG-uh-boo)

something that creates worry
or is upsetting (noun)

For many people, spiders are a huge
bugaboo. They rarely hurt people and
actually help us by catching and eating
bugs that can harm us. But according
to some studies, more than half of
people surveyed are afraid of them.

Words at Work

Not sure what to be when you grow up? We've got you covered! Check out these working words and start leaning the tools of the trade.

JULY 5
Animator
(AN-uh-may-ter)

an artist who creates animated cartoons (noun)

Michiyo Yasuda was a Japanese *animator* who helped create award-winning cartoon movies for Studio Ghibli and other movie studios. She was known for her bold use of color and received an Animation Achievement Award at the Japanese Movie Critics Awards in 2011.

JULY 6
Cosmetologist
(kahz-muh-TAH-luh-jist)

a person who offers beauty treatments for hair, skin, and nails (noun)

Madam C. J. Walker is known as the first Black woman self-made millionaire in the United States. She made her fortune in the early 1900s as a successful *cosmetologist* who created hair and makeup products specifically for Black customers.

JULY 7
Aviator
(AY-vee-ay-ter)

a person who flies airplanes, helicopters, or other types of aircraft (noun)

During a state dinner at the White House, the famous *aviator* Amelia Earhart offered to take First Lady Eleanor Roosevelt on a private airplane ride. The women snuck away, and Earhart flew them from Washington, DC to Baltimore, Maryland, while still wearing formal evening clothes.

JULY 8
Haberdasher

(HAB-er-dash-er)

someone who sells men's clothing and hats (noun)

John Hetherington was a British *haberdasher* in the 1700s who is often credited with designing the first top hat. It is reported that Hetherington had to pay a fine after people fainted at the unusual sight of his top hat.

JULY 9
Entrepreneur

(ahn-truh-pruh-NER)

an individual who creates a new business and takes on financial risks in order to do so (noun)

In 1975, an American *entrepreneur* named Steve Jobs started brainstorming for a new computer company in his parents' garage. That company became Apple Inc, one of the most successful computer and tech companies of all time. The family's house and garage were designated a Historical Resource in 2013 by the Los Altos Historical Commission in California.

JULY 10
Volcanologist

(vahl-kuh-NAH-luh-jist)

a scientist who studies volcanoes (noun)

Dr. Keith Rowley is a *volcanologist* who studied volcanic eruptions in the Caribbean Islands and created safety plans for nearby communities. He went on to become the prime minster of Trinidad and Tobago.

JULY 11

Heyday

• • • • • • • • • •

(HAY-day)

the time when someone or something is most successful, popular, etc. (noun)

The Little Tramp was a character created by actor and filmmaker Charlie Chaplin. In the *heyday* of the silent film era, the character's signature derby hat, cane, toothbrush mustache, and silly charm became instantly recognizable and brought Chaplin worldwide fame.

Mausoleum

· · · · · · · · · · · · ·

(maw-suh-LEE-um)

a large tomb (noun)

The *mausoleum* of Qin Shi Huang, the first emperor of China's Qin dynasty, is the country's largest preserved site. The burial site was discovered in 1974 when farmers found clay shards that led to the discovery of the ancient tomb and thousands of life-size statues now known as the Terra-Cotta Army.

Pizzazz

• • • • • • • • •

(puh-ZAZ)

a quality or style that is exciting
and interesting (noun)

Elton John is a British singer-songwriter
who started his career as a glam rocker in
the early 1970s. His performances were
full of *pizzazz*, and he became known for his
theatrical style, energetic stage presence,
and flashy clothing like rhinestone-encrusted
sunglasses and suits with glitter-fringed trim.

GEESE

A. B.

JULY 14

Nickelodeon

• • • • • • • • • • • • • • • •

(nik-uh-LOH-dee-un)

an early movie theater that often
charged five cents for admission (noun)

Nickelodeons were popular with middle-
and working-class families in the early
1900s because of the affordable price. The
theaters usually showed films that were only
ten or fifteen minutes in length and included
early documentaries, comedies, and dramas.

189

sin cos tan

$\frac{\sqrt{3}}{3}$ $x^2 = x \times x$ $\frac{x}{\sin x}$

$\sqrt{123}$ $\pi = 3.14$

$2x$ $60°$ x

$30°$

$x\sqrt{3}$

$\frac{\sqrt{2}}{2}$ $= \ln\left|t\right|\frac{x}{2}$

$\int \frac{dx}{\sin x} = \ln\left|t\right|\frac{x}{2}$

$\frac{x}{y}$

$\begin{cases} 6x^2 - 2x + x \\ 2x_3 - 3x = \\ 2x_1 + 4 \end{cases}$

?

JULY 15

Hypothesis

• • • • • • • • • • • • •

(hye-PAH-thuh-suss)

a possible explanation for
an observed event (noun)

Since the 1800s, the city of Yoro,
Honduras, has experienced an odd
annual weather event where hundreds
of fish rain down from the sky and onto
the streets after severe thunderstorms.
Some scientists have formed a *hypothesis*
that the fish are transported into the
air by a waterspout (a small column of
rapidly swirling air in contact with a water
surface). Another, less exciting idea is
that fish swimming in underground
streams wash up on the street
during heavy rains.

JULY 16

Marine
• • • • • • • • •
(muh-REEN)

of or relating to the sea or ocean (adjective)

An estimated 50-80 percent of all life on
Earth is *marine* life. All the oceans combined
contain over 70 percent of the living space
on the planet, but less than 20 percent of
that space has been explored by humans.

Panacea

• • • • • • • • • •

(pan-uh-SEE-uh)

something that will make everything about a situation better (noun)

Not long ago, diseases caused by bacteria, most of which are easily treated now, were major causes of death. In 1928, scientist Alexander Fleming discovered a mold that killed bacteria. He isolated the active ingredient, which proved to be the very first antibiotic medicine, the groundbreaking *panacea* we call penicillin.

Loggerheads

• • • • • • • • • • • • •

(LAW-ger-heds)

in a state of strong disagreement—used
in the phrase *at loggerheads* (noun)

In 2015, people around the world were at
loggerheads over a picture of a dress from
the Internet. While some people saw the
dress as striped with black and blue, others
saw it striped with gold and white. Experts
say the disagreement may have been caused
by how different people perceive colors.

Pulchritude

• • • • • • • • • • • •

(PUL-kruh-tood)

having a pleasing physical
appearance (noun)

Oscar Wilde's novel, *The Picture of
Dorian Gray*, is about a young man
who becomes so obsessed with his
own *pulchritude* that he trades his
soul for eternal beauty. In the story,
Dorian's portrait ages while he
remains forever young and beautiful.

JULY 20

Akimbo
• • • • • • • • •

(uh-KIM-boh)

spread apart in a bent position (adjective)

Swimmer syndrome is a disease found in puppies and kittens that
makes their limbs weak, causing them to splay out and often preventing
the animal from standing or walking. Instead, afflicted animals will
lie on their chest and try to move in a way that resembles a turtle
swimming, its legs *akimbo*. Fortunately, physical therapy can help,
and the animal is usually able to attain normal movement as it grows.

Fruit

Take a big bite out of these juicy words!

JULY 21
Tamarind
•••••••••
(TAM-uh-rind)

the fruit of the tamarind tree consisting of an oblong brown pod containing one to twelve flat seeds embedded in a brownish, sticky, acidic pulp (noun)

The *tamarind* tree is one of the most important food sources for Madagascar's ring-tailed lemurs. The lemurs eat both the leaves and fruit of the tree, which grow at different times of year and together provide nearly 50 percent of their diet.

JULY 22
Durian
••••••••
(DUR-ee-un)

a large oval tasty but foul-smelling fruit with a prickly rind (noun)

Due to its strong smell, *durian* is banned from public transportation in Thailand, Japan, and Hong Kong.

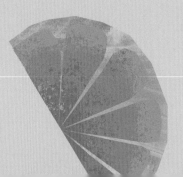

JULY 24
Quandong
●●●●●●●●●
(KAWHN-dahng)

a red, round pitted fruit, similar to a peach, with a tart taste and large, edible seed that grows on shrubby trees in Australia (noun)

The *quandong* tree is a partially parasitic plant that attaches to the roots systems of other plants and steals their nutrients.

JULY 23
Black currant
●●●●●●●●●●●●●
(BLAK-ker-unt)

the aromatic edible black berries of a European perennial currant (noun)

During World War II, shipments of citrus fruits to Great Britain nearly ground to a halt. Prime Minister Winston Churchill's government promoted the cultivation of *black currants* to keep citizens from getting scurvy. This native fruit is heavy in vitamin C, which prevents the deadly disease.

JULY 25
Pitaya
●●●●●●●
(puh-TYE-uh)

a large red, yellow, or pink oval fruit that has leathery skin with prominent scaly spikes and juicy flesh with many tiny black seeds native to Central and South America and Mexico (noun)

Pitaya is commonly called "dragon fruit" in English due to its spiky exterior.

197

JULY 26

Opulent
• • • • • • • • •
(AH-pyuh-lunt)

very luxurious and expensive (adjective)

While most of France lived in poverty,
King Louis XIV spent a great deal of
taxpayer money in the 1600s to build the
opulent Palace of Versailles. The palace
features lavish gardens, fountains, a
private zoo, and more than 2,000 rooms.

JULY 27

Mulch
• • • • • • • •

(MULCH)

a material (such as straw, leaves, or small pieces of wood) that is spread over the ground in a garden to protect the plants, help them grow, and stop weeds from sprouting (noun)

When trees die, many parts of the tree can be broken down and used for other purposes. Tree branches are often pulverized into a nutrient-rich *mulch* that protect plants from the harsh winter elements.

JULY 28

Zeppelin
· · · · · · · · · · ·
(ZEP-uh-lun)

a large aircraft without wings that floats because
it is filled with gas and has a rigid frame inside
its body to help keep its shape (noun)

When the Empire State Building was being built, investors
announced that the building's height would be increased
to allow *zeppelins* to dock at the very top. When the first
zeppelin attempted this feat in 1931, it only docked for three
minutes due to 40 mile per hour (64 kilometer per hour)
winds and caused a major traffic jam on the street below.
The plan for zeppelin docking was eventually scrapped.

JULY 29

Minuscule
• • • • • • • • • • •

(MIN-uh-skyool)

very small (adjective)

Discovered in 2009, the smallest
amphibian in the world is a frog that
measures just seven millimeters long.
The creature is so *minuscule* that several
could fit on the surface of a dime.
Named *Paedophryne amanuensis*, it is the
tiniest known animal with a backbone.

JULY 30

Karaoke
• • • • • • • • • •

(kair-ee-OH-kee)

a form of entertainment in which
a device plays the music of popular
songs and people sing the words to
the songs they choose (noun)

Many bars offering *karaoke* in the Philippines
have removed Frank Sinatra's "My Way" from
their playbooks because singing it has led to
fighting. One reason may be because some
people there consider it to be an arrogant song.
However, many of the fights occurred after
someone sang out of tune, so the violence
could also be due to poor performances.

Sprocket

• • • • • • • • • •

(SPRAH-kut)

a wheel that has a row of teeth around its edge which fit into the holes of something (such as a bicycle chain) and cause it to turn when the wheel turns (noun)

Traditional cameras use rolls of photosensitive film with holes along the sides. A fresh roll of film starts out on one side of the camera. The photographer pushes a lever that turns a set of *sprockets*. As they turn, the sprockets catch the holes in the sides of the film, unrolling a piece into position to capture an image. After the picture is taken, the photographer pushes the lever again, and the sprockets advance the film, rolling the new photo to the other side of the camera and a fresh piece of film into place to capture the next image.

Story of the month

I have no idea what to be when I get older, and adults make you choose too fast! I had an *ephemeral* career as "class clown," but my teacher told me that doesn't count. I don't want to end up with a boring job, and I'm very *intransigent* about it. I want a career with *pizzazz*!

I could become a fruit *entrepreneur* who starts a business shipping fruit around the world! I'd travel to Australia to harvest *quandong*, or trade *pitaya* and *black currant* in Nigeria for fresh *tamarind*. I'd even sell *durian* if I could put up with the smell. Maybe I could become a celebrity *cosmetologist* who gives a relaxing face *lavation* to actors before their close-ups. Or I could be the owner of a wild *karaoke* bar with guests singing and dancing, limbs all *akimbo*. It would be neat to be a cemetery caretaker, looking for ghosts in *mausoleums* and planting flowers in the *mulch*. But perhaps I should become something more exciting, like a *volcanologist* studying an island lava flow from my *marine* vessel.

Sometimes I feel like I missed out on the *heyday* of certain jobs. I could have been an *aviator* of a *zeppelin*, but no one really flies those anymore. I could have been an *animator* for old cartoons showing in a *nickelodeon*. If I could go back in time, maybe I could have been a *haberdasher* of *opulent* clothes fit for a royal with *pulchritude*, or a watchmaker carefully placing *minuscule sprockets* where they belong.

I can't seem to decide what to do when I grow up and it is becoming a **bugaboo** for me. My parents and I are at **loggerheads** over what I should become. But why do I need a job at all? I have one **hypothesis**. If we could live our lives and enjoy all of our passions, not just one, that would be quite the **panacea**.

Hear the story read aloud.

Aug

ust
· · · · · · · · ·

AUGUST 1

Disperse
• • • • • • • • • •
(dih-SPERSS)

to distribute or spread widely (verb)

A rainbow appears when sunlight passes through a raindrop and is *dispersed* into its full spectrum of colors, sending red, orange, yellow, green, blue, indigo, and violet light into the sky.

AUGUST 2

Taboo
● ● ● ● ● ● ● ●

(tuh-BOO)

not acceptable to talk about or do (adjective)

Judy Blume's bestselling novel, *Are You There God? It's Me, Margaret*, has been adored by readers for decades. Published in 1970, the story includes subjects that many adults considered *taboo* at the time, such as puberty, buying bras, and interfaith marriage. Despite being banned by many libraries, the book continues to sell and has become a modern classic.

Accumulate
• • • • • • • • • • • • • •

(uh-KYOO-myuh-layt)

to gather or acquire (something)
gradually as time passes (verb)

Mansa Musa was a 14th-century ruler of the
kingdom of Mali, the largest and richest empire
in West African history. Musa *accumulated* so
much wealth that he crashed the Egyptian
economy for 12 years after visiting the country
and paying for things with solid gold.

Killjoy
• • • • • • • •

(KIL-joy)

a person who spoils other people's fun or enjoyment (noun)

Oliver Cromwell, the leader of the English government in the 1650s, was a strict Puritan leader. Some thought him a *killjoy* because he did not approve of Christmas celebrations. During his rule, soldiers were sent through the city to seize and destroy any special food prepared for the holiday.

Monopoly
• • • • • • • • • • •
(muh-NAH-puh-lee)

complete control of all goods and
services in a particular market (noun)

Marcus Licinius Crassus was an ancient
Roman general and politician who made
his wealth in many dishonest ways. He
gained a *monopoly* on firefighting in Rome.
Because he controlled all firefighting
services, Crassus made homeowners pay
him huge bribes. If they refused to pay,
Crassus would let their houses burn down.

Ambidextrous

• • • • • • • • • • • • • • •

(am-bih-DEK-strus)

able to use the right and left
hands equally well (adjective)

Very few people—about 1 percent of the
population—are born *ambidextrous*. Still,
the ability to use both hands equally
well can be learned over time. In a 1919
article, Serbian inventor Nikola Tesla
wrote, "I am ambidextrous now," though
he admitted to being born left-handed.

Bugs

Don't let these creepy, crawly words get under your skin.

AUGUST 8
Botfly
• • • • • • • •
(BAHT-flye)

a small, hairy fly that lays eggs inside the bodies of large mammals (noun)

When *botflies* lay eggs in the nostrils of sheep, they can cause a nervous condition called "blind staggers," where the host animal walks with uneven steps and appears to be blind.

AUGUST 7
Cicada
• • • • • • • •
(suh-KAY-duh)

a large black insect with long, transparent wings that spends most of its life underground and has a loud mating call (noun)

Some species of *cicada* stay underground for 13 to 17 years before maturing into adulthood and emerging all at once in a large group called a "brood."

AUGUST 9
Millipede
• • • • • • • • •
(MIL-uh-peed)

an invertebrate animal with a long body composed of many segments, most of which have two pairs of legs (noun)

Millipedes are born with only a few pairs of legs and grow many more pairs during their lifetime. One adult species of white millipede from California boasts up to 750 legs.

AUGUST 10
Katydid
• • • • • • •
(KAY-tee-did)

a large green grasshopper usually with organs on the forewings of the males that produce a loud shrill sound (noun)

Male *katydids* attract females by rubbing their forewings together to create sound. While it may sound like all the bugs "sing" in unison, scientists have learned that each male is trying to be the first to sing a new note. Studies have shown that female katydids select the first male in a group that broadcasts a new tone, even if it was only 70 milliseconds faster than the other males.

AUGUST 11
Weevil
• • • • • •
(WEE-vuhl)

a small beetle with an elongated snout (noun)

There are more than 60,000 species of *weevil* in the world. Weevils are herbivores that often feed on the same plant species their entire lives. Many weevils are named after the foods they eat, including the Rice Weevil and the Wheat Weevil.

AUGUST 12
Mantis
• • • • • •
(MAN-tuhss)

a large green insect that feeds on other insects and holds its prey in its forelimbs (noun)

This formidable bug is often called a "praying *mantis*" because it appears to draw its limbs together in prayer when it latches onto prey. But mantises are not peaceful insects. Female mantises are known to kill and eat their male partners.

Aardvark
• • • • • • • • • • • •
(AHRD-vahrk)

a large African animal with a long
nose that eats ants and other insects
using its elongated tongue (noun)

The *aardvark* is revered by several African tribes,
including the Mangbetu, who admire it for its
bravery. Some people wear aardvark teeth
on bracelets to serve as good luck charms.

Odoriferous

• • • • • • • • • • • • • • • •

(oh-duh-RIF-uh-russ)

very smelly (adjective)

Scientists conducted a study where they played different kinds of music to cheese as it aged. A panel of judges found that cheese exposed to hip-hop music was more *odoriferous* than cheese exposed to classical, rock, or techno music.

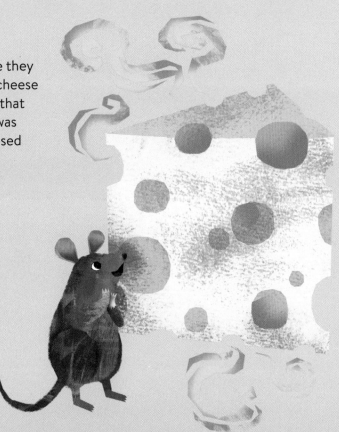

Igloo

• • • • • •

(IG-loo)

a temporary winter dwelling made of blocks of snow or ice in the form of a dome (noun)

Despite being cold, snow is actually a great insulator of heat. Even if temperatures outside drop as low as −49 degrees Fahrenheit (-45 degrees Celsius), inside an *igloo*, body heat can keep the temperature as high as 61 degrees Fahrenheit (16 degrees Celsius).

Abacus
• • • • • • • • •
(AB-uh-kus)

a device used for counting and calculating by sliding small balls or beads along rods or in grooves (noun)

The average *abacus* can easily fit on a tabletop, but Ajit Singh from India decided to make one that was much, much larger. In 2011, Ajit built an abacus that measured 22 feet (6.7 meters) by 10.5 feet (3.2 meters) and weighed 262 pounds (118 kilograms), the largest one in existence.

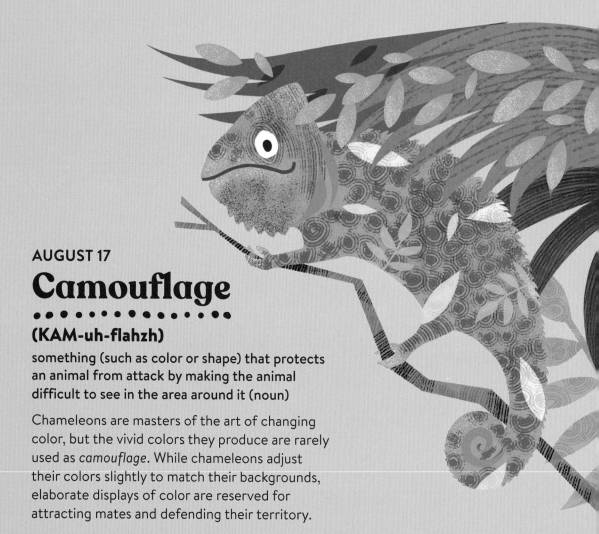

AUGUST 17

Camouflage
· · · · · · · · · · · · ·
(KAM-uh-flahzh)

something (such as color or shape) that protects
an animal from attack by making the animal
difficult to see in the area around it (noun)

Chameleons are masters of the art of changing
color, but the vivid colors they produce are rarely
used as *camouflage*. While chameleons adjust
their colors slightly to match their backgrounds,
elaborate displays of color are reserved for
attracting mates and defending their territory.

AUGUST 18

Odyssey

(AH-duh-see)

a long journey full of adventures (noun)

Inspired by Jules Verne's novel, *Around the World in 80 Days*, journalist Nellie Bly undertook an *odyssey* in 1889 to travel around the world in even less time. Bly traveled alone by ship, train, and rickshaw, and she made it around the world in only 72 days.

221

Fortnight
· · · · · · · · · · · ·
(FORT-nyte)

a period of 14 days: two weeks (noun)

Pope Urban VII was Pope of the Roman Catholic Church in 1590 for less than a *fortnight*. He died of malaria just 12 days after becoming Pope, making it the shortest reign in the history of the Church.

Chitchat

• • • • • • • • • • • •

(CHIT-chat)

friendly conversation about things
that are not very important (noun)

Small talk, like discussing the weather
or weekend plans, can be an important
social tool. Not only does *chitchat*
make people happier, but it can also
deepen connections, build trust, and
increase the ability to solve problems.

Comeuppance

· · · · · · · · · · · · · · · · · · · ·

(kum-UP-unss)

punishment that someone
deserves to receive (noun)

In 1974, Elvis Presley's manager, Colonel Tom
Parker, convinced the rock star to produce
an album of talking instead of singing called
Having Fun with Elvis on Stage. Parker's
idea was to keep a majority of the profits
for himself. Luckily, he got some form of
comeuppance when the album tanked.

Pareidolia
· · · · · · · · · · · ·

(pair-eye-DOH-lee-uh)

the tendency to see a specific
or meaningful image in a
random visual pattern (noun)

Pedra da Gávea is a 2,700-foot-high
(823-meter-high) mountain in Brazil's
Tijuca Forest. Because of *pareidolia*,
some people say they can see a
person's face, complete with a hat or
helmet, in the large rock at the peak.

Space Words

Blast off to another galaxy with these galactic words!

AUGUST 24
Gibbous
• • • • • • • •
(JIB-us)

with more than half but not all of the apparent disk illuminated—used to describe a view of the Moon or a planet (adjective)

As the Moon orbits the Earth, the parts of the Moon that face the Sun are illuminated. When more than half the Moon faces the Sun, it creates a *gibbous* Moon, which occurs right before and after a full Moon.

AUGUST 23
Asteroid
• • • • • • • • •
(AST-uh-royd)

a small, rocky body that orbits the Sun (noun)

On November 25, 2005, JAXA (Japan Aerospace Exploration Agency) landed the Hayabusa spacecraft on the *asteroid* Itokawa. It was the first space mission to collect surface material from an asteroid and bring it back to Earth.

AUGUST 25
Extraterrestrial
• • • • • • • • • • • • • •
(ek-struh-tuh-RESS-tree-ul)

coming from or existing outside the planet Earth (adjective)

In his book *Extraterrestrial*, astrophysicist Avi Loeb discusses a strange giant object called 'Oumuamua that passed through our Solar System in 2017. Due to the object's brightness and bizarre flight pattern, Loeb believes that 'Oumuamua may be an *extraterrestrial* visitor from an alien civilization.

AUGUST 26
Lunar
• • • • • •
(LOO-nuhr)

of, or related to, the Moon (adjective)

NASA astronaut Harrison Schmitt was a part of the Apollo 17 mission that landed on the Moon on December 11, 1972. As he and a fellow astronaut explored the Moon's surface, dust stuck to their boots, suits, and tools. When Schmitt returned to the spacecraft, he removed his helmet and his nose got stuffed up. That's how he discovered he was allergic to *lunar* dust.

AUGUST 27
Nebula
• • • • • • •
(NEB-yuh-luh)

a large cloud of gas or dust in outer space (noun)

The closest *nebula* to Earth, the Helix Nebula, is made of gas given off by a dying star.

AUGUST 28
Supernova
• • • • • • • • •
(soo-per-NOH-vuh)

the bright explosion of a star at the end of its life that can be one trillion times brighter than the Sun (noun)

Some heavy elements, like iron, are only created in *supernovas*. Humans typically have between three and four grams of iron in their bodies, which means we all carry the remains of space explosions.

AUGUST 29

Deciduous

• • • • • • • • • • • • •

(dih-SIJ-uh-wus)

having leaves that fall off
every year (adjective)

Deciduous trees prepare for winter
hibernation by shutting down their
food production systems and reducing
the amount of chlorophyll in their
leaves. Chlorophyll is a chemical that
helps plants make food and gives them
their green color. When trees reduce
the amount of chlorophyll, other
chemicals become more noticeable,
and this is what gives autumn leaves
their red, orange, and yellow colors.

AUGUST 30

Phenomenon
· · · · · · · · · · · · · · · ·
(fih-NAH-muh-nahn)

an exceptional, unusual, or abnormal
person, thing, or occurrence (noun)

Under the right conditions, Horsetail Falls in
Yosemite National Park in the United States
gives off a glow resembling lava or falling fire,
a natural *phenomenon* referred to as "firefall."

230

Temerity

• • • • • • • • • • •

(tuh-MAIR-uh-tee)

**unreasonable confidence or boldness
in the face of danger (noun)**

Kitty O'Neil was a Hollywood stuntwoman known
for holding a land-speed record of 618 miles per
hour (994 kilometers per hour) while driving a three-
wheeled rocket through the desert. Her *temerity*
allowed her to succeed at death-defying stunts and
earned her the title of "the fastest woman in the world."

Story of the month

• • • • • • • • • • • • • • • • • • • •

Captain's log: Day 4,852—It has been a *fortnight* since my last log. Our spaceship, the USS *Huxley*, is nearing the end of our long *odyssey* after passing through an *asteroid* field to arrive above a new planet. Let me just say, we have *accumulated* some unusual observations. We have seen *gibbous lunar* views and an explosive *supernova*. We even saw a *nebula* that looked like an *igloo*, but it may have just been my own *pareidolia*.

Meanwhile, the crew is engaging in careless *chitchat* and losing focus while on duty. I don't want to be a *killjoy*, nor do I want fun to be *taboo* on the ship, but we must remain committed to the mission. I have had to reprimand the crew many times. I would rather their *comeuppance* be a stern warning from me than the breakdown of our ship. *Temerity* in space could lead to disaster. We are carrying precious living cargo from Earth, including *cicadas*, *botflies*, *weevils*, *mantises*, and *katydids*. We also have larger creatures, like *aardvarks*, which always try to eat the bugs. I need my crew to focus and keep these animals safe. They are supposed to be experts in zoology and astrophysics, but I doubt my crew could even use a simple *abacus*.

Now for the most exciting discovery—I am stunned at a *phenomenon* occurring on the planet below our spaceship. Here, we have discovered *extraterrestrial* life! In addition to *odoriferous* plants and *deciduous* trees, we found a bug-like creature that *disperses* an acidic gas every few days. This creature looks like a *millipede* with hundreds of small legs and two giant *ambidextrous* arms it uses to hunt prey. This morning, we discovered that the creature uses *camouflage* to blend into its surroundings. It also appears to have a *monopoly* on the planet's mushroom population—every mushroom we can see is hollowed out to make room for the creature's eggs. I wonder if this little critter is smart enough to communicate. We will have to wait and see. Until next time...

Hear the story read aloud.

Sept

ember

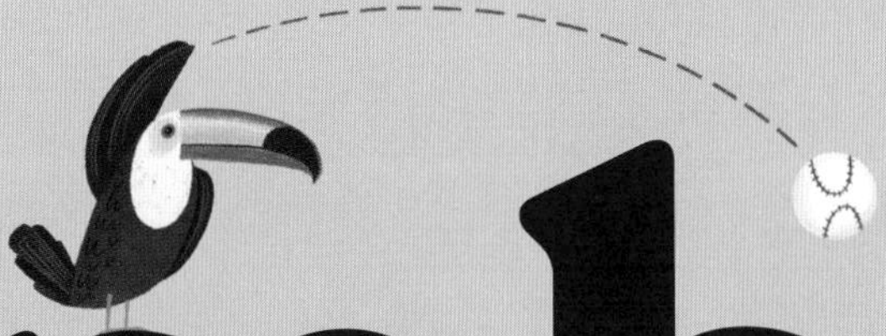

SEPTEMBER 1

Cuckoo

● ● ● ● ● ● ● ● ●

(KOO-koo)

a type of bird that lays its eggs in the nests of other birds and has a call that sounds like its name (noun)

To chime the hour, a cuckoo clock opens a small wooden door, and a wooden *cuckoo* emerges to cry "cuckoo" once for one o'clock, twice for two o'clock, and so on. It is thought that these clocks were originally made in the 1600s with wood from the Black Forest in southwest Germany.

Ostentatious

(ah-stun-TAY-shuss)

attracting attention, admiration,
or envy in an obvious way (adjective)

The Sultan of Brunei, Hassanal Bolkiah, has a
collection of approximately 7,000 cars, including
an *ostentatious* Rolls-Royce Silver Spur II stretch
limousine. The entire vehicle is plated with 24-carat
gold and has an estimated price of $14 million.

SEPTEMBER 3

Trajectory

· · · · · · · · · · · · · · ·

(truh-JEK-tuhr-ree)

the curved path an object follows as it moves
through the air or through space (noun)

On July 25, 1931, Mildred "Babe" Didrikson
Zaharias set the world record in baseball for
longest throw by a woman. With a *trajectory*
of 296 feet (90 meters), the distance was
almost as long as the Statue of Liberty is tall.

SEPTEMBER 4

Unique

· · · · · · · · · ·

(yoo-NEEK)

being the only one of its kind (adjective)

Everyone knows that no two persons'
fingerprints are the same, but few people
are aware that scientists have discovered
the same for tongue prints. Every person
has a *unique* pattern on their tongue.

Regenerate

· · · · · · · · · · · · · ·

(rih-JEN-uh-rayt)

to grow again after being
lost or damaged (verb)

Of all the organs in a human body, the
liver is the only one that has the incredible
ability to *regenerate*. If 25-65% of the liver
is damaged or removed, the organ can
fully grow back to its original size.

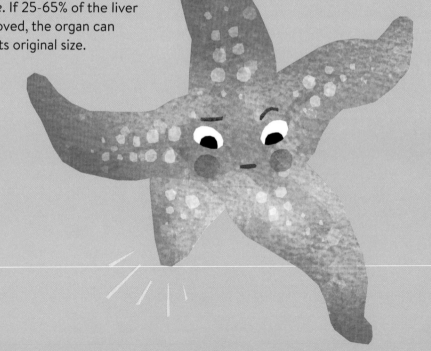

SEPTEMBER 6

Cornucopia
• • • • • • • • • • • • • •
(kor-nuh-KOH-pee-uh)

a container that is shaped like a horn and is full of fruit and vegetables; a great amount or source of something (noun)

Across cultures, the *cornucopia* has become a symbol of abundance and the harvest season and is also known as the "horn of plenty." The ancient Greeks believed the horn was broken off the head of a baby goat and used to feed Zeus, one of their gods, by his nurse when he was a baby. According to legend, an endless supply of nourishment flowed from the broken horn, giving it its name.

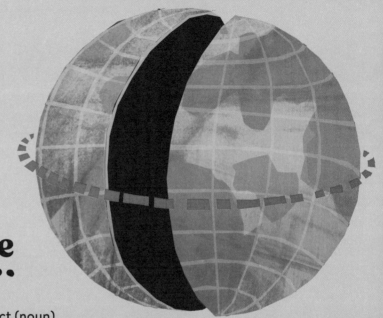

Hemisphere

• • • • • • — • • • • • •

(HEM-uh-sfeer)

half of a sphere or round object (noun)

The Earth can be divided into *hemispheres* in two different ways: vertically and horizontally. The Equator divides Earth horizontally into the Northern and Southern Hemispheres. The Prime Meridian divides the Earth vertically into Eastern and Western Hemispheres. Africa is the only continent in the world that crosses both the Equator and the Prime Meridian, meaning it rests on all four areas of the Earth—East, West, North, and South.

Quid pro quo

● ● ● ● ● ● ● ● ● ● ● ● ● ● ● ●

(kwid-proh-KWOH)

something that is given to you or done for you in return for something you have given or done for someone else (noun)

The relationship between chimpanzees and the African nutmeg plant involves something of a *quid pro quo*. Chimps eat the nutmeg to calm stomachaches. As the seed of the nutmeg plant moves through a chimp's body, the tough outer layer is stripped away by stomach acids. When chimps pass the seed in their stool, it can grow into a new tree because the outer layer has been removed.

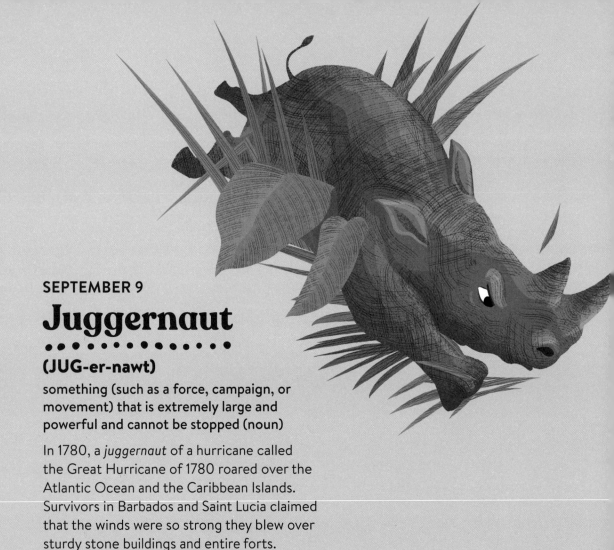

SEPTEMBER 9

Juggernaut
· · · · · · · · · · · ·
(JUG-er-nawt)

something (such as a force, campaign, or movement) that is extremely large and powerful and cannot be stopped (noun)

In 1780, a *juggernaut* of a hurricane called the Great Hurricane of 1780 roared over the Atlantic Ocean and the Caribbean Islands. Survivors in Barbados and Saint Lucia claimed that the winds were so strong they blew over sturdy stone buildings and entire forts.

SEPTEMBER 10

Agenda

· · · · · · · · · ·

(uh-JEN-duh)

a list of things to be considered or done (noun)

Composer Ludwig van Beethoven often kept to
the same schedule most days. After getting up at
dawn, his *agenda* consisted of carefully counting
sixty beans for his cup of coffee and working for
several hours. His midday meal came next, followed
by a long walk outdoors. He spent the evening
hours at the theater, in the company of friends,
or reading newspapers at taverns. He was in bed
by 10:00 PM, ready to do it again the next day.

Crochet

• • • • • • • • • •

(kroh-SHAY)

a method of making cloth or clothing by using a needle with a hook at the end to form yarn into interwoven loops (noun)

Polish fiber artist Olek often uses *crochet* to create site-specific works of art. Olek travels across the world creating giant yarn "cozies" that cover buildings and large monuments. She once covered an entire house in Sweden with pink crocheted fabric and knitted a head-to-toe sweater for the Charging Bull statue in New York City's financial capital, Wall Street.

Adjacent
• • • • • • • • • •
(uh-JAY-sunt)

close or near; sharing a border, wall, or point (adjective)

In 2019, archeologists discovered the remains of a board game from 1,800 years ago near the site of an ancient Roman bathhouse. Oddly, the board game was being used as a floorboard in an *adjacent* building. Historians believe that someone at the bathhouse broke the board game, and the broken pieces were used to build the floor of a nearby structure.

Vivid Vocabulary

Brighten your world by swapping common colors for these handsome hues.

SEPTEMBER 13
Cerulean
• • • • • • • •
(suh-ROO-lee-un)
a blue color, like the sky or the sea (noun)

In 2000, the color and graphic company Pantone choose *cerulean* as its "Color of the Year." The company called the color "tranquil" and "peaceful."

SEPTEMBER 14
Puce
• • • • •
(PYOOSS)
a dark red (noun)

In 18th-century France, clothing colored *puce* became fashionable in the court of Louis XVI. The brownish-red color kept clothes from showing much dirt and grime which allowed royals to look their best.

SEPTEMBER 15
Flaxen
• • • • • • •
(FLAK-sun)
resembling flax in pale soft straw color (adjective)

In Charles Dickens's book, *David Copperfield*, the title character describes his crush on a young girl "with a round face and curly *flaxen* hair."

SEPTEMBER 16
Cyan
••••••
(SYE-an)

a greenish-blue color (noun)

Cyan is one of the main colors of ink used in printing, along with black, yellow, and magenta. When combined, these four inks can create the thousands of colors you find in books and magazines.

SEPTEMBER 17
Periwinkle
•••••••••••
(PAIR-ih-wing-kul)

a pale color somewhere between blue and violet (noun)

Periwinkle was a common color in ancient Egyptian jewelry, often made from a bluish, purplish stone called *lapis lazuli.*

SEPTEMBER 18
Chartreuse
•••••••••••
(shahr-TROOZ)

a bright yellow-green color (noun)

According to legend, the color *chartreuse* is named for a bright green drink created by a 16th-century alchemist who promised good health and a long life to those who drank it.

249

SEPTEMBER 19
Dilute
• • • • • • •
(dye-LOOT)

to lessen the strength of something
by mixing it with something else (verb)

In the 1600s, the bubonic plague killed about fifteen to twenty percent of London's population. Doctors believed people caught the disease by breathing in deadly gases, so they tried to *dilute* the bad air with something just as strong to prevent people from getting sick. They advised patients to trap any gas they passed in containers and have these "fart jars" ready to sniff in case they were exposed to plague-filled air. (The plague was actually spread by biting fleas.)

Scuttlebutt

• • • • • • • • • • • •

(SKUT-ul-but)

talk or stories about someone
that may not be true (noun)

In 1692, Salem, Massachusetts, was
swept up in hysteria as townsfolk
accused one another of practicing
witchcraft, sparking a series of court
cases known as the Salem Witch
Trials. In court, tests were performed
to determine if people were witches,
such as checking the accused for
moles that were considered
"witches' marks." Unsupported gossip
and *scuttlebutt* were also permitted
as evidence, and ultimately 19
people were executed before the
community came to its senses.

SEPTEMBER 21

Aboveboard
• • • • • • • • • • • •

(uh-BUV-bord)

open, honest, and legal; in a
straightforward manner (adjective)

Major soccer leagues have introduced
a system called VAR—video assistant
referee—in order to be more
aboveboard in making calls. In addition
to the referees on the field, an official
watches camera feeds from a booth
and can bring the referees over to
review any play that might be in doubt.

SEPTEMBER 22

Contented

• • • • • • • • • • • •

(kun-TEN-tud)

happy and satisfied: showing or feeling contentment (adjective)

When cats are *contented*, they often make a low, vibrating sound called purring. Scientists are still not sure how cats produce a purr. But they've found that some larger cats, like cheetahs and bobcats, also make a purring sound.

SEPTEMBER 23

Inflation
• • • • • • • • • • • •
(in-FLAY-shun)

a continual increase in the price of goods and services (noun)

In 1920s Germany, *inflation* became so bad that in some restaurants, waiters would stand on chairs every half hour and announce the new prices for their menu. Some people found that if they sat down and ordered a meal, by the time the food came, the price had changed and they might no longer be able to afford it.

Perspire
• • • • • • • • •
(per-SPYRE)

to sweat through the pores as a result of heat, stress, or physical exertion (verb)

Sweating is the body's way of regulating temperature. When you *perspire*, the moisture on your skin evaporates, which cools the skin. The average person has two to four million sweat glands on their body.

Predict

● ● ● ● ● ● ● ● ● ●

(prih-DIKT)

**to say that something will
happen in the future (verb)**

Neptune was the first planet to be
discovered using mathematics. Working
separately, astronomers John Couch
Adams and Urbain-Jean-Joseph Le Verrier
each noticed that the planet Uranus was
being pulled slightly off its normal orbit and
guessed that the cause was an undiscovered
planet. With some calculations, they figured
out the planet's location and size. A short
time later, astronomer Johann Gottfried
Galle pointed his telescope at the spot
Adams and Le Verrier had pinpointed.
And there was Neptune, right where
they had *predicted* it would be!

SEPTEMBER 26

Juxtapose

· · · · · · · · · · · · · ·

(JUK-stuh-pohz)

to place (different things) together
in order to create an interesting effect
or to show how they are the same
or different (verb)

When people *juxtapose* two things that
are very different, they often say it's
like "comparing apples and oranges."
However, apples and oranges are both
edible fruit that contain similar amounts
of calories and vitamin C. In most cases,
juxtaposing two unlike things is more
like comparing apples and helicopters.

SEPTEMBER 27

Rustic

• • • • • • • •

(RUSS-tik)

made of rough wood (adjective)

The National Park Service in the United States uses a style called "*rustic* architecture" when they build structures such as visitor centers and rain shelters. Rather than stand out from the landscape, park structures are built with simple logs and stones meant to blend into their natural surroundings.

Spurn

· · · · · · · ·

(SPERN)

to refuse to accept someone or something that you do not think deserves your respect, attention, or affection (verb)

Bessie Coleman was determined to become a pilot. Despite being *spurned* by American flight schools because she was Black and a woman, she persevered and learned to fly planes in France. Coleman became one of the most popular pilots in the world and went on to perform magnificent stunts all over the United States.

SEPTEMBER 29
Kerplunk
• • • • • • • • • • • • •
(ker-PLUNK)

with a loud dull sound; with a thud (adverb)

In 1956, the city of Miami, Florida, had to pay a woman $300 after a coconut fell *kerplunk* from a city-owned tree and landed on her foot, causing injuries.

SEPTEMBER 30
Conclave
· · · · · · · · · · · ·

(KAHN-klayv)

a private or secret meeting or group (noun)

The Independent Order of Odd Fellows is a *conclave* tracing back to the 1700s. Members meet in lodges and are encouraged to improve themselves and help those in need. According to legend, members encounter skeletons in secret rituals to remind them of their own mortality. Many of these skeletons are fake, but real human bones have been found in some older lodges. The exact role of these skeletons remains a mystery to those outside the organization.

Story of the month

· ·

The Superminati is a **conclave** of the world's greatest superheroes. The meeting is a secret to all except the superheroes, but the proceedings are always **aboveboard**. The location is in a jungle that could make even the fittest **perspire**. From the outside, the headquarters of the Superminati looks like a hermit's hut. But **juxtaposed** with that **rustic** exterior is the inside—a strangely large, futuristic space with a **cornucopia** of high-tech screens, computers, gadgets, and devices.

When all are in attendance, the room is filled with bright and colorful costumes bordering on **ostentatious**. There are caped crusaders in every shade of color, including **cerulean**, **cyan**, **puce**, **chartreuse**, and **periwinkle**. Volatus, who can chart a perfectly accurate **trajectory** that carries him across entire **hemispheres** in just minutes, is usually in attendance, along with Regina Tiv, who has the **unique** power of **regenerating** parts of her body. And then there's Zip—a superfast, super-strong **juggernaut** of a person, capable of running on water. As you can imagine, the behind-the-scenes **scuttlebutt** is always very entertaining.

As the heroes have made the world safer, however, the **agenda** for the Superminati has become **diluted** with "boring" problems like **inflation** and political **quid pro quos**. In this year's meeting some members even fell asleep during the first presentation.

But the quiet didn't last long. Seemingly from nowhere, a *cuckoo* sound interrupted the meeting. Then another. And another. And many, many more. Where could it have been coming from? After all, the headquarters was sealed. Someone in the room must have been to blame. Accusations came thick and fast. Heroes began accusing one another and *spurned* each other's claims of innocence. Finally, a voice called out and the fighting stopped. In the corner, *crocheting* with *flaxen* wool, sat Futura, a superhero with the power to *predict* the future. She spoke calmly, saying "Zip, open the cabinet *adjacent* to your chair." He did. And what do you suppose happened? That's right, a cuckoo clock fell out, *kerplunk*, and the noise stopped. "Thank goodness that's over," said a *contented* Futura. She picked up her yarn. "Let's continue the meeting."

Hear the story read aloud.

ober
· · · · · · · · · · · · ·

OCTOBER 1

Ignite
• • • • • • • •
(ig-NYTE)

to set on fire or cause a fuel to burn (verb)

Did you know that every car on the road has a fire burning inside it? A gasoline-powered engine mixes fuel with oxygen and *ignites* the mixture with a device called a spark plug. By controlling the amount of oxygen in the mixture, the engine can capture the energy from the burning fuel to make the car go and still keep the fire under control so it doesn't burn up the car.

OCTOBER 2

Acuncture

· · · · · · · · · · · · · · · · ·

(AK-yuh-punk-cher)

a method of relieving pain or curing illness by placing needles into a person's skin at particular points on the body (noun)

In traditional medicine in China, where *acupuncture* originated, the technique is used to help balance one's "Chi" (life force or flow of energy). The inserted needles are meant to redirect the flow of energy through proper pathways. Scientists have studied acupuncture, and many believe that it relieves pain because the needles help stimulate muscles and nerves in a way that boosts the body's natural painkillers.

OCTOBER 3
Vice versa
· · · · · · · · · · · · · ·
(VYCE-VER-suh)

used to say that the opposite of a
statement is also true (adverb)

Alexander Hamilton and Aaron Burr, two
founding fathers of the United States,
were bitter rivals during and after the
Revolutionary War. Hamilton hated Burr
and *vice versa*. The rivalry came to a
head when Burr challenged Hamilton to
a duel. The two faced off in Weehawken,
New Jersey, where Burr shot Hamilton,
who died from his wounds.

OCTOBER 4
Slapstick
• • • • • • • • • • • •
(SLAP-stik)

comedy that involves physical action
(such as falling down or hitting people) (noun)

The Three Stooges were an American comedy
team that performed *slapstick* in the early to
mid-1900s. The trio of comedians—named Moe,
Larry, and Curly (and occasionally others)—were
known for their physical comedy, such as falling
off chairs, cracking eggs on their heads, and
throwing pies in one another's faces.

OCTOBER 5
Schmooze
•••••••••••••
(SHMOOZ)

to talk with someone in a friendly way, often in order to get some advantage for yourself (verb)

In 2020, Hungarian artist Andi Schmied posed as a billionaire and *schmoozed* realtors to gain access to some of New York City's most elite penthouses. She brought a camera with her to photograph views from the luxury apartments and turned those pictures into a book.

Alter

• • • • • •

(AWL-ter)

to change partly but not completely (verb)

In 2020, Princess Beatrice married Edoardo Mapelli Mozzi in a gown that had been previously worn by her grandmother, Queen Elizabeth II. The dress was *altered* to fit Beatrice and large, puffy sleeves were added.

Musical Words

The notes on a written sheet of music tell a musician what sounds to play. These musical words tell a musician exactly *how* to play a piece of music.

OCTOBER 8
Fortissimo
• • • • • • • • • • •

(for-TISS-uh-moh)

very loudly (adverb)

When two letter *f*'s (ff) appear in sheet music, musicians play *fortissimo*.

OCTOBER 7
Crescendo
• • • • • • • • • • •

(kruh-SHEN-doh)

a gradual increase in loudness (noun)

The abbreviation "cresc." or an elongated angle bracket (<) written in sheet music tell musicians to play louder for a *crescendo*.

OCTOBER 9
Pianissimo
• • • • • • • • • • •

(pee-uh-NISS-uh-moh)

very softly (adverb)

Two letter *p*'s (pp) tell musicians to play *pianissimo*.

OCTOBER 10
Staccato
• • • • • • • • •

(stuh-KAH-toh)

in a manner that keeps the musical notes short and separate from one another (adverb)

When a dot appears above a note, it means the note is *staccato*.

OCTOBER 11
Legato
• • • • • • • •

(lih-GAH-toh)

smooth and connected (adjective)

A curved line above or below a row of notes symbolizes a *legato* passage where musicians play fluidly with notes blending into one another.

273

OCTOBER 12

Superfluous
• • • • • • • • • • • • • •
(soo-PER-floo-uss)

beyond what is needed; not necessary (adjective)

A vast collection of ocean debris known as the Great Pacific Garbage Patch floats in the North Pacific Ocean. Debris builds over time because humans produce *superfluous* amounts of single-use plastics. Scientists agree that eliminating our use of disposable plastics and switching to biodegradable resources is the best way to keep the mess from getting even bigger.

OCTOBER 13

Mangle

• • • • • • • •

(MANG-gul)

to injure or damage (something or someone) severely by cutting, tearing, or crushing (verb)

In 1986, a canvas by abstract painter Barnett Newman called "Who's Afraid of Red, Yellow and Blue III" was shown at the Stedelijk Museum in Amsterdam, the Netherlands. The painting of bold colors and straight lines upset many in the art world who felt that Newman's art was so simple, anyone could paint it. One angry person even *mangled* the painting by slashing it with a blade.

275

Scholar

• • • • • • • • • •

(SKAH-ler)

**a person who devotes their
life to study (noun)**

The Islamic Golden Age was a period
of great advancement in medicine,
technology, mathematics, and culture
from the eighth to thirteenth centuries.
With a high value placed on education,
scholars were encouraged to acquire
knowledge in many fields of study.

OCTOBER 15

Whodunit
• • • • • • • • • • • •

(hoo-DUN-it)

a novel, play, or movie about a murder where the audience is given clues to the identity of the murderer but doesn't find out for sure until the end (noun)

Agatha Christie wrote over 66 detective novels in her life and is often considered a master of the *whodunit*. She was once at the center of her own mystery, as well, when she disappeared for 11 days after her first husband asked for a divorce. The story made the front page of newspapers and caused thousands of volunteers to try and find her, eventually leading to her discovery in a hotel.

OCTOBER 16

Topsy-turvy
· · · · · · · · · · · · · ·
(tahp-see-TER-vee)

upside down; in or into great
disorder or confusion (adverb)

According to archaeological records, in the
year 536 AD, a storm of dust clouds caused a
disaster that wiped out much of the population
of Europe and the area that is now Turkey.
Scientists now believe these dust clouds may
have been caused by a volcanic eruption.
Because sunlight was blocked by volcanic ash,
the weather was turned *topsy-turvy* for 12 to
18 months with a drop in temperature that
resulted in icy summers and severe winters.

278

OCTOBER 17

Derive
• • • • • • • •

(dih-RYVE)

to take or get from a source (verb)

While modern marshmallows are made from sugar, corn syrup, and gelatin, thousands of years ago they were *derived* from the mallow plant that grows wild in marshes. Some of the first people to enjoy the gooey treat were ancient Egyptians, but back then it was rare and reserved for gods and royalty.

Pugnacious
· · · · · · · · · · · · · ·

(pug-NAY-shuss)

showing a readiness or desire
to fight or argue (adjective)

Humans are unusual among animals partly
because we can think logically. Recently,
French scientists put forth a theory
called the "argumentative theory of
reasoning." It states that our ability to
reason evolved to win arguments. This
means that our ability to think logically
may be a new version of an old need to
win fights with other *pugnacious* people.

Noodge
• • • • • • • • • •

(NOOJ)

to pester or bother (verb)

Benjamin Franklin is considered a founding father of the United States, but his friends may have considered him a pain. Franklin took joy in winning unimportant arguments. He once *noodged* Noah Webster, the author of the first American dictionary, to replace six letters in the alphabet. Webster was also an advocate for spelling reform, but did not use Franklin's letters in his dictionaries.

Mnemonic

• • • • • • • • • • • •

(nih-MAH-nik)

something (such as a word, a sentence, or a song)
that helps people remember something else
(such as a rule or a list of names) (noun)

A *mnemonic* can be a useful trick for remembering
the planets in our solar system in the order of
their distance from the Sun. The first letters of
every word in the sentence, "**M**y **V**ery **E**xcellent
Mother **J**ust **S**erved **U**s **N**achos," match the first
letters of planets **M**ercury, **V**enus, **E**arth, **M**ars,
Jupiter, **S**aturn, **U**ranus, and **N**eptune.

Rickety

• • • • • • • •

(RIK-uh-tee)

weak or unstable and likely to break (adjective)

In 1998, a marble bust made by French artist Edmé Bouchardon in 1728 was discovered in a *rickety* shed on an industrial park in Scotland. The bust of Sir John Gordon, valued at almost $2 million, was found being used as a door stop. It has since been restored and shown in museums around the world.

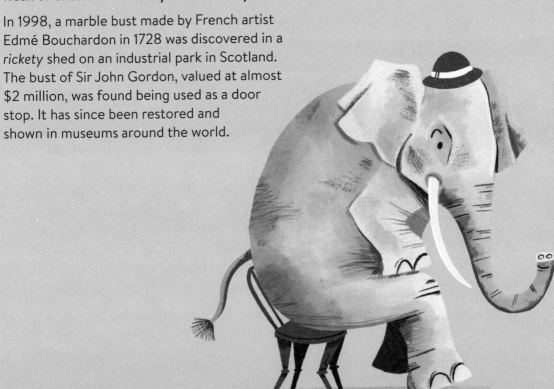

Edible

• • • • • • • •

(ED-uh-bul)

able to be eaten (adjective)

Archeologists have discovered pots of honey in ancient Egyptian tombs that have remained unspoiled. If honey stays completely sealed, it can last for thousands of years and still be *edible*!

OCTOBER 23

Malaise
• • • • • • • • • • ••

(muh-LAYZ)

a slight or general feeling of not being healthy or happy (noun)

In addition to a stuffy nose, a frequent symptom of the common cold is *malaise*. But why do people seem to get more colds during wintertime? Some blame it on the drop in temperature but weather has nothing to do with it. Instead, because sick people usually stay inside, it puts them in close range with other people who are seeking the warmth of indoors. Combine that with reduced air flow, and you get the conditions for colds to spread more easily than they do in warmer weather.

Spooky Words

These terrifying words will send a shiver down your spine.

OCTOBER 24
Apparition
• • • • • • • • • •

(ap-uh-RISH-un)

the unusual or unexpected sight of a person or thing, especially a ghost (noun)

Some visitors to the Tower of London claim to have seen the *apparition* of Anne Boleyn, the former Queen of England, who was beheaded in 1536 by her husband King Henry VIII. According to legend, her ghost has been seen both with and without a head.

OCTOBER 26
Eerie
• • • • • •

(EER-ee)

mysterious in a spooky or frightening way (adjective)

The National Film and Sound Archive in Canberra, Australia, is often called one of Australia's most haunted places. The building originally opened to the public in 1931 as the Institute of Anatomy and contained hundreds of skeletons and mummies. Today, staff members claim to hear *eerie* noises coming from areas of the building where dissection laboratories used to be.

OCTOBER 25
Macabre
• • • • • • • • •

(muh-KAHB)

involving death or violence in a way that is strange, frightening, or unpleasant (adjective)

Archaeologists in Bulgaria made a *macabre* discovery when they dug up a skeleton from the 1200s with a stake through its heart. Experts believe that some early European cultures feared vampires and drove stakes through the hearts of the dead to prevent them from returning as the undead.

OCTOBER 27
Hobgoblin
• • • • • • • •

(HAHB-gahb-lun)

a small, mythical creature
that creates mischief (noun)

In Welsh mythology, *hobgoblins*
called "the Bwbach" (BOO-bach)
are friendly, mischievous creatures
who live with families and perform
household chores in exchange for
fresh cream. The term *Bwbach*
means "little scare" in Welsh
because these hobgoblins are
known for their pranks.

OCTOBER 28
Gruesome
• • • • • • • •

(GROO-sum)

causing horror or disgust (adjective)

In Southeast Asian cultures, the
gruesome ghost of a young woman's
severed head haunts the countryside
at night. According to legend, the
severed head—called "Krasue" in
Thailand—flies through the night sky
with its internal organs hanging out,
painting the ground red with blood.

OCTOBER 29
Phantasm
• • • • • • • • •

(FAN-taz-um)

an illusion, apparition, or ghost that is
a figment of the imagination (noun)

Researchers at the Committee for Skeptical Inquiry, an
organization that uses science to investigate the paranormal,
revealed that *phantasm*s may just be a trick of the eye. Studies
show that people who are tired or performing mindless tasks
often "see" things out of the corner of their eye, but these
things are actually our brains projecting random images.

Establish

(ih-STAB-lish)

**to successfully start or make something
that did not exist before (verb)**

Japan is home to many of the world's oldest businesses.
Ichimonjiya Wasuke is a candy store in Kyoto that was
established in the year 1000 AD. The store is known
for its history as well as its delicious rice cakes called
aburi mochi that are believed to ward off sickness and evil.

Boffo

• • • • • • •

(BAH-foh)

extremely good or successful (adjective)

In the 1930s, an editor named Abel Green started work at *Variety*, a weekly newspaper reporting on Hollywood. Green initiated a new kind of writing for *Variety* known as "slanguage," full of slang and peculiar words and phrases. In *Variety*'s slanguage, a strong opening weekend in Japan for the movie *Transformers*, directed by Michael Bay is expressed in the headline "Bay's 'Bots *Boffo* in Japan."

FIRST PLACE

Story of the month

It was a night unlike any other at the haunted disco. At Club Bones, *macabre apparitions* danced with *eerie hobgoblins* to songs played *fortissimo*. A *crescendo* in the music brought all the ghosts to the dance floor, where they bobbed and weaved to the *staccato* beats. Attendees danced, chatted, and tumbled into one another in a show of *slapstick* fun. But the night soon turned from a *schmoozing* event into a confusing one!

Everything was going great until the tunes started playing *pianissimo*. Suddenly, the DJ booth *ignited* in sparks and the music cut out entirely. The whole place was sent *topsy-turvy*, which *altered* the mood and brought on a serious *malaise*. Then the spooky guests discovered that someone had *mangled* the cables to the DJ booth. The party turned into a *whodunit* as guests tried to figure out who cut the cables. The *pugnacious* mummies blamed the zombies for the interruption and *noodged* them to confess, while the werewolves accused the vampires and *vice versa*. A trio of witches, who had been performing *acupuncture* off to the side, threw down their needles and accused the trolls of the crime.

It was starting to look like something *gruesome* might happen. Then Detective Specter stepped forward. He was a *scholar* of mystery who *derived* his skill for remembering ghostly events from the use of *mnemonics*. He *established* a theory. He pointed out that none of the haunted guests ate food, so the mice that lived in the walls of the disco were probably very hungry. The mice came out looking for dinner, saw the spaghetti-like cords, and chomped away thinking they were *edible*. Detective Specter shined a light into the mouse hole to reveal three mice with fat bellies full of speaker wire. Mystery solved!

Meanwhile, someone had discovered a *rickety* cart in the closet along with an old boombox and a *superfluous* amount of music from Count Dracula's 30,000 song collection. Finally, as if the whole ordeal were merely a *phantasm*, new tunes flowed from the boombox, the monsters floated back to the dance floor swept up by the *legato* music, and the party was once again *boffo*.

Hear the story read aloud.

Nove

mber

NOVEMBER 1

Charisma
· · · · · · · · · · · ·
(kuh-RIZ-muh)

a special charm or appeal that causes
people to feel attracted and excited by
someone (such as a politician) (noun)

For a decade, Henry Winkler played the
character famously known as "the Fonz"
on the show *Happy Days* set in Milwaukee,
Wisconsin. The tough-guy-with-a-heart-
of-gold character oozed *charisma*, making
the Fonz an instant hit with TV viewers.
In 2008, a bronze statue of the Fonz was
placed on the Riverwalk in Milwaukee.

NOVEMBER 2

Buoyant

• • • • • • • • •

(BOY-unt)

capable of floating (adjective)

The Dead Sea in Israel has up to nine times more salt than the world's oceans, which makes a person naturally *buoyant* in the waters. If you were to jump into the Dead Sea and lean back, your whole body would immediately pop up to the surface.

Aloof

• • • • • •

(uh-LOOF)

not involved with or friendly toward other people (adjective)

The poet Emily Dickinson became famous only after her death. The *aloof* writer lived a reclusive life in her family's home where she wrote bundles of poetry and hundreds of letters in secret. When she died, her writings were discovered and published to much acclaim. She is now considered one of the great figures of American literature.

Erratic
• • • • • • • •
(ih-RAT-ik)

acting, moving, or changing in ways that
are unexpected or usual (adjective)

Cloudy with a Chance of Meatballs is a picture book written by
Judi Barrett and illustrated by her husband, Ron Barrett, that
came out in 1978. The classic children's story tells the tale of
a town called Chewandswallow where the weather's timing is
predictable—always at breakfast, lunch, and dinner—but the
elements are food instead of rain or wind. As the weather
gets more *erratic*, the people of Chewandswallow are forced
to deal with hamburger storms and mashed potato snow.

Medicinal

· · · · · · · · · · · · ·

(muh-DISS-un-ul)

having healing properties (adjective)

Ketchup was originally made with mushrooms or fish until the 1800s, when an American doctor named John Cook Bennett started a tomato craze that swept the United States. Bennett claimed tomatoes had *medicinal* benefits so could cure a variety of ills. At Bennett's suggestion, tomatoes were added to many foods, including ketchup, making the condiment more like the one eaten today.

Inherit

• • • • • • • • •

(in-HAIR-ut)

to receive something from someone who had it previously (verb)

Humans get goosebumps because of a trait that was *inherited* from our animal ancestors. When animals are cold or feel threatened, tiny muscles make their hair stand up to keep them warm or make them look bigger to scare off potential attackers. Although modern humans no longer have the hairy bodies of our ancestors, our skin still stands up with goosebumps when we get cold or feel strong emotions such as excitement, anger, or fear.

NOVEMBER 7
Palindrome
• • • • • • • • • • • • • •
(PAL-un-drohm)

a word, verse, sentence, or a number that reads the same backward or forward (noun)

Try reading these *palindromes* from left to right, and then again from right to left:
- Was it a car or a cat I saw?
- Sit on a potato pan, Otis.
- Too bad I hid a boot.

NOVEMBER 8

Yo
●●●●
(YOH)

used especially to attract someone's attention, as a greeting, or in response to a greeting (interjection)

"Yo, Adrian!" was a phrase popularized by the character Rocky Balboa, played by Sylvester Stallone in the Rocky movies. The greeting "Yo" had been slang among Italian Americans in South Philadelphia for some time. After the movies, "Yo" was later embraced by the language of hip-hop culture of the 1970s and 80s. Today, it has become a common greeting across America.

Landlocked

• • • • • • • • • • •

(LAND-lahkt)

surrounded by land (adjective)

Of all the *landlocked* countries in the
world, only three of them are located
entirely within another country's borders.
Lesotho is a small country situated entirely
within South Africa, while San Marino and
Vatican City are both located within Italy.

Pyretic
• • • • • • • • •

(pye-RET-ik)

marked by or caused by a fever (adjective)

When you have a fever, your body temperature spikes past its normal temperature, which for most humans is between 97- and 99-degrees Fahrenheit (36- and 37-degrees Celsius). Most fevers only increase your body temperature by a few degrees, but one *pyretic* man in 1980 arrived at the hospital with a 115-degree Fahrenheit (46-degree Celsius) fever . . . and lived to the tell the tale.

Pruritus

• • • • • • • • • •

(proo-RYE-tuss)

severe itching of the skin (noun)

Have you ever tried to resist scratching
an itch? It's a good idea to try because
scratching actually makes *pruritus* worse.
But it can be almost impossible to resist
the soothing sensation that scratching
an itch creates in the brain . . . before
the itch comes roaring back again.

Whippersnapper

· ·

(WIP-er-snap-er)

a young person who annoys older people by being very confident and acting like someone important (noun)

Greta Thunberg is a young climate change activist who has become a leading voice in the fight against the climate crisis. In 2019, she spoke at the UN climate conference and criticized politicians and corporations for relying on young people to fix the crisis instead of making changes they need to make fast enough. While Greta's critics may consider her a *whippersnapper*, millions of people have joined her cause.

Flowery Language

Take time to stop and smell these fragrant words, fresh from the garden.

NOVEMBER 13
Grevillea

(gruh-VIL-ee-uh)

a large genus of Australian shrubs and trees usually with showy orange and red flowers (noun)

Grevillea flowers bloom all year round, especially important in hot climates like Australia and New Guinea. Beetles, flies, bees, and birds drink the flower's sweet nectar and help pollinate the plant throughout the year.

NOVEMBER 14
Thistle

(THISS-ul)

a prickly plant with large, tubular flowers (noun)

The *thistle* is the national flower of Scotland. The Most Ancient and Most Noble Order of the Thistle is an award given to those who have made an outstanding contribution to Scottish culture.

NOVEMBER 16
Edelweiss

(AY-dul-vyce)

a small mountain herb with dense, wooly, white flowers (noun)

Edelweiss is native to the Alps in Southern Europe. A stirring song called "Edelweiss" appears in the movie musical *The Sound of Music*, which tells the tale of a family's escape from the Nazis during World War II.

NOVEMBER 15
Foxglove
• • • • • • • • • •
(FAHKS-gluv)

a tall plant that has many white or purple bell-shaped flowers growing on its stem (noun)

Foxglove is dangerous to eat, containing a chemical compound that can bring on confusion and change the perception of color. Some art critics suspect that Vincent van Gogh's "yellow period"—several years when the artist painted in yellow tones—was brought on by exposure to foxglove.

NOVEMBER 17
Dogwood
• • • • • • • • • •
(DAWG-wood)

a tree or shrub with clusters of small flowers, often with pink, white, or red petals (noun)

Dogwoods are often planted in people's yards for their beautiful flowers. But the tree is used for herbal medicine as well. For centuries people have used its bark and leaves to treat pain, fevers, and dizziness.

NOVEMBER 18
Chrysanthemum
• • • • • • • • • • • • • •
(krih-SANTH-uh-mum)

a plant that has brightly colored flowers and that is often grown in gardens (noun)

First cultivated in China, *chrysanthemums* were traditionally used as a edible herb in foods and teas. The flower quickly spread worldwide and was used in a wider variety of ways. In Japan, the flower was used on the Emperor's official seal. In Europe, chrysanthemums are often brought to funerals and gravesites.

307

NOVEMBER 19
Widget
• • • • • • • • •
(WIJ-ut)
any small mechanical or
electronic device (noun)

In the 1980s, computer programs could only
have one application open at a time. The
team at Apple Computers changed that. They
created a program of simple tools, originally
called "desk ornaments," that required so
little processing power they could run in the
background of another program. A calculator,
a clock, sticky notes, and a puzzle game
became the very first computer *widgets*.

Thermal

· · · · · · · · · · ·

(THER-mul)

of, relating to, or caused by heat (adjective)

The Eiffel Tower in Paris was built to be able to sway in the wind, but the sun can also make it move. When the side that faces the sun heats up, it expands, causing the top of the tower to shift as far as seven inches (17 centimeters) away from the sun. The 1,063-foot (324-meter) iron structure can also grow up to an additional six inches (15 centimeters) in height on warm days due to the same *thermal* expansion.

Harsh

(HAHRSH)

**unpleasant and difficult to accept
or experience (adjective)**

Camels have three eyelids. Two of the eyelids have
eyelashes that protect their eyes from the *harsh*
blowing sands of the desert. The third eyelid,
which moves from side to side, is much thinner
and works to protect and clean off the eyes.

Caustic

• • • • • • • • ••

(KAW-stik)

able to destroy or burn something by chemical action; very harsh (adjective)

Sodium hydroxide, a compound known primarily for its *caustic* properties, is used to manufacture everyday products like paper, soaps, aluminum, cleaners, and detergents. It is even used in food production for curing olives or browning Bavarian-style pretzels, giving them their characteristic crunch.

Moniker

• • • • • • • • •

(MAH-nih-ker)

a name or nickname (noun)

Comedian Whoopi Goldberg's name is actually a *moniker*. Born Caryn Elaine Johnson, her nickname comes from a practical joke toy. In 2006, she was quoted in the *New York Times*, "When you're performing on stage, you never really have time to go into the bathroom and close the door. So if you get a little gassy, you've got to let it go. So people used to say to me, 'You are like a whoopee cushion.' And that's where the name came from."

Concoction
● ● ● ● ● ● ● ● ● ● ● ●

(kun-KAHK-shun)

something (such as a food or drink) that is made by mixing together different things (noun)

In 1905, an 11-year-old boy from California named Frank Epperson accidentally created a new *concoction* when he mixed water with a sugary soda powder and left it outside one cold night. The next day, he ate the frozen mixture off the wooden stirrer. Epperson called his discovery an "Epsicle" and sold the sweet treat in his neighborhood. He later changed the name to "Popsicle."

Pivotal
• • • • • • • • • •
(PIV-uh-tul)

very important (adjective)

On July 5, 1996, Dolly the sheep was born. As the first cloned mammal ever to be created from an adult cell, her birth caused a worldwide sensation and was a *pivotal* moment in cloning technology. Dolly's existence proved that the cell of an adult mammal could be manipulated to produce an entirely new living mammal.

Parapet

• • • • • • • • •

(PAIR-uh-put)

a low wall at the edge of a platform, roof, or bridge (noun)

Parapets might look decorative, but they have practical purposes. They first appeared on buildings across England after the Great Fire of London in 1666 because they slow the spread of fire between houses. Modern parapets on roofs are also designed to protect them from winds.

Kiosk

• • • • • • • •

(KEE-ahsk)

a small store in a building or on the street where things (such as newspapers or candy) are sold (noun)

Haines of Sloane Square is the oldest news *kiosk* in London, selling newspapers, drinks, and more. Located a mile from Buckingham Palace, the business has been run by the same family ever since it opened in 1892. Princess Diana is rumored to have been a regular customer as a teenager, stopping to flip through fashion magazines during the time she worked at a nursery school nearby.

NOVEMBER 28
Hobnob
• • • • • • • • •
(HAHB-nahb)

to spend time with someone (such as a famous
or wealthy person) in a friendly way (verb)

Two con men were jailed after it was discovered they
had tricked wealthy people out of more than 55 million
euros. Using a silicone mask that made one of them look
like the French defense minister, the men *hobnobbed*
with politicians and business leaders over a video
conference platform and asked them for money for
government operations. The men approached more than
150 prominent people including the King of Belgium.

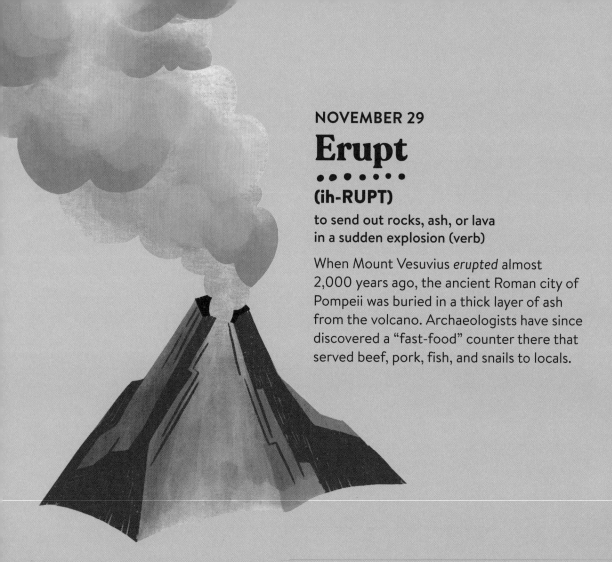

Erupt
• • • • • • •
(ih-RUPT)

**to send out rocks, ash, or lava
in a sudden explosion (verb)**

When Mount Vesuvius *erupted* almost
2,000 years ago, the ancient Roman city of
Pompeii was buried in a thick layer of ash
from the volcano. Archaeologists have since
discovered a "fast-food" counter there that
served beef, pork, fish, and snails to locals.

NOVEMBER 30
Harangue
• • • • • • • • • •
(huh-RANG)

a forceful or angry speech (noun)

If you forget to finish your homework
or crack jokes during class, your
teacher may deliver a *harangue*
about slacking off in school.

Story of the month

Something was wrong with the Queen. While she normally had the **charisma** to keep even the dullest conversation **buoyant**, lately she was acting **aloof** and **erratic**. Her weekly speeches from the top of the castle were normally lively and pleasant. But now, she began to **erupt** with **harsh harangues** from the **parapets**. Her daughter, Cleona, **hobnobbed** with her mother and the royal elites of the **landlocked** kingdom enough to know that there was a problem. The **pivotal** moment came when the Queen grew **pyretic** and could no longer speak. Her skin broke out in a rash and she experienced severe **pruritus**. Try as they might, with their magic **widgets** and spells full of **palindromes**, the court wizards could not fix the Queen's **thermal** stress, nor her itchiness.

However, Cleona spent much of her time studying and knew that her mother's illness could not be cured with spells, but with something **medicinal**. "I can heal her! I just need some help!" Cleona exclaimed, but the royal court ignored her, calling her a **whippersnapper**. Cleona knew that her mother's passing meant she would **inherit** the throne, but she did not want that to happen any time soon. The Princess would save her mother, no matter what.

Cleona snuck out of the castle and made her way to the nearby town. She wore plain clothes and used a **moniker** to move about the market unnoticed. She found a **kiosk** selling all different types of plants. Cleona had made a list of what she needed—some mountain **edelweiss**, desert **grevillea**, leaf of **dogwood**, **chrysanthemum**, **foxglove**, and a pinch of **thistle**.

"**Yo**!" she called to the merchant and handed him the list. Cleona received the plants from the merchant and raced back to the castle. She ground the plants down to a fine powder, mixed it with river water, and rushed the **concoction** to her mother. The Queen drank the **caustic** potion which burned as it went down her throat. Suddenly, the Queen's fever broke. Long live the Queen!

Hear the story read aloud.

Dece

mber

Vamoose
• • • • • • • • • • •

(vuh-MOOSS)

to depart quickly (verb)

The people of Winnipeg, Canada, know what it's like to have to *vamoose* for their lives. In the spring of 1950, the Red River, which runs through the city, jumped its banks. Snow melt and heavy rain surged across the city, leaving parts of it covered by as much as 15 feet (4.5 meters) of water. More than 100,000 people (about one-third of the city's residents) were evacuated and couldn't return to their homes for almost two months.

DECEMBER 2

Descendant
· · · · · · · · · · · · ·
(dih-SEN-dunt)

a person, plant, or animal related
to an individual or group that lived
at an earlier time (noun)

Rats can produce new litters of baby rats in
only 21 days. If ideal conditions allow, then
in three years, just two rats can theoretically
produce half a billion *descendants*.

DECEMBER 3

Swarm

• • • • • • • •

(SWORM)

a large number of living or nonliving things grouped together, usually in motion (noun)

In some places, fireworks are being replaced by a large *swarm* of drones because drones are safer to operate. Thousands of drones are fitted with bright LED lights and controlled by a computer program that allows them to fly together to create colorful shapes and intricate patterns.

DECEMBER 4

Abominable

• • • • • • • • • • • • • • • •

(uh-BAH-muh-nuh-bul)

very bad or unpleasant (adjective)

King Henry VIII earned the reputation of being a tyrant largely based on the *abominable* behavior he exhibited during his reign. He led a series of largely unsuccessful, bloody wars and executed two of his six wives.

DECEMBER 5
Satire
• • • • • • • •
(SAT-ire)

humor that shows the weaknesses or bad qualities of a person, government, society, etc. (noun)

Practiced throughout history, *satire* is a form of artistic expression that allows people to laugh at and understand different aspects of society. It can take many forms—novels, plays, films, TV shows, music, and memes. Many places recognize the importance of poking fun at well-known leaders and institutions, and some countries, including Germany and Italy, even protect satire in their constitutions.

DECEMBER 6

Venture

· · · · · · · · · · ·

(VEN-sher)

to go somewhere that is
unknown or dangerous (verb)

Sacagawea was a Lemhi Shoshone woman who
played a critical role in the 1804–1806 Lewis and
Clark Expedition to explore lands that the United
States had recently bought from France. The
only woman in the group, Sacagawea served as
an interpreter as the expedition *ventured* across
the American West to the Pacific Ocean. (She
carried her baby on her back the whole time.)

329

Wearable Words

These fashionable words never go out of style.

DECEMBER 7
Anorak

• • • • • • • •

(AN-uh-rak)

a usually pullover hooded jacket long enough to cover the hips (noun)

The Inuit of Greenland make traditional *anoraks* from animal hides and treat them with fish oil to make them waterproof.

DECEMBER 8
Pince-nez

• • • • • • • •

(panss-NAY)

a pair of glasses with a nose clip instead of earpieces (noun)

During the American Civil War, eyeglass manufacturer John Jacob Bausch responded to metal shortages by creating a style of *pince-nez* made of rubber.

DECEMBER 9
Balaclava

• • • • • • • •

(bal-uh-KLAH-vuh)

a warm hat that covers the head, neck, and most of the face (noun)

During the Crimean War, British troops wore *balaclavas* to keep their face, heads, and ears warm in the bitter cold.

DECEMBER 10
Cummerbund
• • • • • • • • • • • •

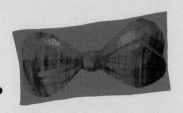

(KUM-er-bund)

a wide piece of cloth (such as silk) that is worn around the waist beneath the jacket of a man who is formally dressed (noun)

The *cummerbund* originated in India and was traditionally worn by men. Today, it is commonly worn at formal events, often with tuxedos.

DECEMBER 11
Knickerbockers
• • • • • • • • • • • •

(NIK-er-bah-kerz)

loose-fitting short pants that gather at the knee or calf (plural noun)

In the 1800s, *knickerbockers* were originally worn by men and boys, but they soon became popular with all sports enthusiasts. Because these pants gathered at the knee, loose fabric couldn't trip athletes or get caught in bicycle spokes. The word was later shortened to *knickers*.

DECEMBER 12
Galoshes
• • • • • • • • •

(guh-LAW-shuz)

tall rubber shoes that are worn over other shoes in wet weather to keep your feet dry (plural noun)

The Indigenous peoples of the Amazon region created *galoshes* centuries ago using sap from rubber trees. Historians aren't sure how they molded the boots, but some believe these early inventors coated their feet with sap and held them over the fire until the sap hardened.

DECEMBER 13
Ruffian
• • • • • • • • • •
(RUH-fee-uhn)

a brutal person; a bully (noun)

In the sci-fi adventure movie *Back to the Future*, the character of Biff is a *ruffian* who bullies the hero, Marty McFly, and his father, George. In one scene, Biff locks Marty in the trunk of his car. Another time, the bully tries to steal money from George.

DECEMBER 14

Physically

• • • • • • • • • • •

(FIZ-ih-klee)

related to or involving the body
or physical form (adverb)

The Australian Coat of Arms features images of a
kangaroo and an emu that serve as symbols of the
country's progress. Neither animal can *physically*
move backward easily. Besides being found only
in Australia, the animals are thought to embody
the Australian motto "Advance Australia."

DECEMBER 15
Whirlybird
• • • • • • • • • • • •
(WER-lee-berd)

helicopter (noun)

The world's first practical helicopter lifted off the ground in Stratford, Connecticut, on September 14, 1939. The *whirlybird* was designed by Igor Sikorsky and built by a division of the United Aircraft Corporation. The first flight was piloted by Sikorsky himself and only lasted a few seconds.

DECEMBER 16

Aft
• • • •
(AFT)

the back of a boat, ship, or airplane (adjective)

On a ship, the terms *aft* and *stern* are often used interchangeably, but there is a difference. "Aft" refers to the rearmost inside (or onboard) part of the ship, while "stern" is the rearmost outside (or offboard) part of the vessel.

Our Daily Bread

Would bread by any other name taste as sweet? Absolutely.

DECEMBER 17
Naan
• • • • • •

(NAHN)

an Indian bread that is round, flat, and soft (noun)

Though *naan* has been around for thousands of years on the Indian subcontinent, the first written mention of the bread can be found in the writings of poet Amir Khusrau. According to his notes, naan was served in the 1300s at the Imperial Court in Delhi for elite members of society.

DECEMBER 18
Challah
• • • • • • •

(HAH-luh)

a bread made with eggs and typically braided or twisted before baking, traditionally eaten by Jewish people on the Sabbath and holidays (noun)

The size, shape, and number of braids in a loaf of *challah* all have different meanings in the Jewish tradition. Often, the dough is braided to form twelve "humps" that represent the twelve tribes of Israel.

DECEMBER 19
Fry bread
• • • • • • • • •

(FRYE-bred)

a fast-cooking bread made by deep-frying, originally created by Indigenous tribes of North Americans, probably in the Southwest (noun)

Fry bread is delicious, but the food has a somber history. In the mid-1800s, the US government forcefully removed the Navajo and other Native American tribes from their homes in present-day Arizona. To prevent starvation, the government provided white flour, sugar, and lard—which the people used to make fry bread. Today, the bread is a staple of many Native American cuisines and a reminder of perseverance over injustice.

DECEMBER 20
Injera
• • • • • •

(in-JAIR-uh)

a flat, spongy bread traditionally made from teff (noun)

Injera is made with the flour of an ancient grass called *teff* that is native to the eastern African countries of Ethiopia and Eritrea. The bread is cooked on a hot skillet and dotted with air bubbles.

DECEMBER 21
Lavash
• • • • • • •

(luh-VAHSH)

a large, thin flatbread with a rough surface caused by air bubbles (noun)

Lavash is an important bread in Armenian cuisine and plays a part in many cultural traditions. At Armenian weddings, lavash is often placed on the bride's shoulder to represent luck, wealth, and new life.

DECEMBER 22
Focaccia
• • • • • • • •

(foh-KAH-chee-uh)

a flat Italian bread usually seasoned with herbs and olive oil (noun)

Different regions of Italy top their *focaccias* with different ingredients. In Liguria, focaccia is often topped with onions, green olives, or anchovies. A sweeter taste can be found in Florence where residents enjoy focaccia topped with grapes.

Tradition

• • • • • • • • • • • •

(truh-DISH-un)

**a belief or custom handed down from
one generation to another (noun)**

In Thailand, people celebrate the Buddhist New
Year (called Songkran) with a festival that is known
as the largest water fight in the world. Throwing
water is believed to wash away bad luck from
the year before. While the *tradition* now often
includes water guns, the holiday was originally
celebrated with families coming together to
pour water over statues of the Buddha.

DECEMBER 24

Caravan

(KAIR-uh-van)

a group of people traveling together (noun)

The Silk Road was an ancient trade route that stretched from China all the way to Europe and parts of Africa. *Caravans* of travelers traded goods and products (not just silk) along the route which helped spread various cultures, inventions, and ideas across the vast area.

DECEMBER 25

Jocular
• • • • • • • •

(JAH-kyuh-ler)

liking to tell jokes; said or
done as a joke (adjective)

Moms Mabley is considered one of
the founders of modern stand-up
comedy. Born Loretta Mary Aiken in
North Carolina, she began working as a
standup comedian, and eventually took
the stage name "Moms Mabley." The
jocular star was a headliner at the Apollo
Theater in Harlem, had hit comedy
albums, and starred in several films.

Knickknack

• • • • • • • • • • • • • •

(NIK-nak)

a small trivial article usually
intended as an ornament (noun)

The *knickknack* salesman was a popular
subject of Chinese court paintings. A
15th-century painting called *The Knickknack
Peddler* shows a merchant with a cart selling
trinkets, toys, and sweet treats to children.

341

DECEMBER 27

Exorbitant

•••••••••••••

(ig-ZOR-buh-tunt)

going far beyond what is fair, reasonable, or expected; too high or expensive (adjective)

While most dog collars are made of leather or nylon, some wealthy pet owners prefer a more *exorbitant* option like the Amour Amour Diamond Dog Collar, which costs $3.2 million. Adorned with 1,600 diamonds set in white gold, it is made of crocodile leather and is the most expensive dog collar in the world.

DECEMBER 28

Fluorescent

• • • • • • • • • • • • • •

(floo-RESS-unt)

able to give off visible light after being exposed to light, heat, or another energy source (adjective)

In 2014, scientists found that some sharks can glow in the dark. The chain catshark and the swell shark use *fluorescent* green shapes in their skin to communicate with one another.

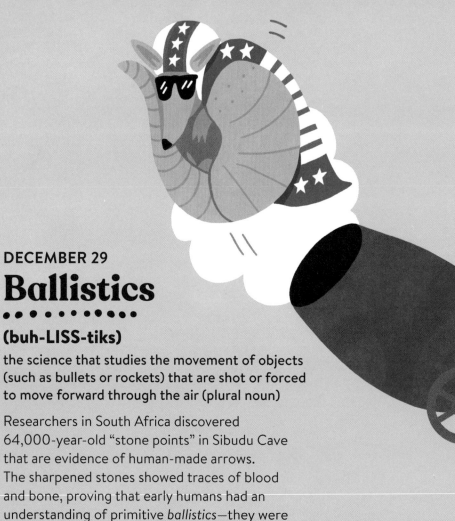

DECEMBER 29

Ballistics

• • • • • • • • • •

(buh-LISS-tiks)

the science that studies the movement of objects (such as bullets or rockets) that are shot or forced to move forward through the air (plural noun)

Researchers in South Africa discovered 64,000-year-old "stone points" in Sibudu Cave that are evidence of human-made arrows. The sharpened stones showed traces of blood and bone, proving that early humans had an understanding of primitive *ballistics*—they were able to launch arrows in the air and hit prey.

Penultimate

· · · · · · · · · · · · · · · · ·

(pih-NUL-tuh-mut)

occurring immediately before
the last one (adjective)

The Beatles' final live concert in August 1966 at
Candlestick Park in San Francisco, California,
was technically their *penultimate* live show.
Thinking it would be their last show, musicians
John Lennon and Paul McCartney brought
cameras out onstage to take photos of the
crowd and of themselves. However, their final
show actually occurred in 1969 on the rooftop
of the Apple Records building in London.

DECEMBER 31
Ebullient
• • • • • • • • • •

(ih-BULL-yunt)

lively and enthusiastic (adjective)

Jazz trumpeter Dizzy Gillespie was known for his dynamic playing, fast tempos, and energetic stage performance. His 1959 album called *The Ebullient Mr. Gillespie* features up-tempo songs that include conga drums.

347

Story of the month

· ·

I have been lucky enough to live the life of an explorer. I've **ventured** across dusty lands and stormy seas to all corners of the globe. Along the way, I've learned valuable lessons. First lesson: approach new people with a **jocular** attitude. I calmed a **swarm** of **abominable ruffians** in the desert by telling funny stories and trading **knickknacks**. This will allow you to make new friends wherever you go.

My second lesson: pack smartly so you don't spend an **exorbitant** amount of money on clothes. You will need outfits for all occasions. Standing at the **aft** deck of a ship gets cold, so if you want to catch a glimpse of the **fluorescent** jellyfish at night, you'll need to pack a warm **anorak**, **balaclava**, and a pair of **galoshes**. But fancy invitations can occur at any moment. I was once invited to sit with the **descendants** of royals at a concert hall and watch the premiere of a new **satire**. Thankfully, I had packed my good pair of **knickerbockers**, a **cummerbund**, and my prescription **pince-nez**.

My third lesson: respect and partake in local **traditions**. I have encountered **caravans** of travelers along my routes and celebrated their holidays, joined in their dances, and dined on their food. Oh yes, I have broken many a bread in my day—**focaccia**, **naan**, **challah**, **fry bread**, **injera**, and **lavash**—and all were delicious.

Now that I am old, not **physically** what I once was, I am planning for my **penultimate** voyage. I am taking off in a new invention called a **whirlybird**, which provides excellent views of the sky! I don't quite understand the **ballistics**, but my crew assures me that this heavy vehicle will fly. Please know that I am not sad, but rather **ebullient** to be taking my second to last trip. Now I must **vamoose** and prepare for my departure. Maybe I'll learn some lessons along the way and take my final trip as an older but wiser adventurer.

Hear the
story read
aloud.

Source Notes

This book's research process was multi-layered. The authors used a wide range of reliable sources for each topic, then fact checkers used additional sources to ensure each fact is correct. In addition, an expert reviewed every topic for accuracy. The result is more sources than there is room to share here. The experts are listed on page 2, opposite the title page. Below is a small sample of the authors' sources for each word.

Hoodwink: Lynch, Patrick. "Catch Me If You Can: The Real Story of Frank Abagnale, Jr.," www.historycollection.com. Ovation: The Kennedy Center. "Leontyne Price," www.kennedy-center.org. Guffaw: Ashish. "Why Does Your Stomach Hurt When You Laugh Really Hard?," www.scienceabc.com. Epiphany: Ballard, Elise. Epiphany: true stories of sudden insight to inspire, encourage, and transform. New York, NY: Harmony Books, 2014. Ad-Lib: Rosen, Jody. "We the Best Forever," www.rollingstone.com. Klutz: Selvin, Claire. "Visitor Damages Antonio Canova Sculpture While Attempting to Take a Selfie," www.artnews.com Mayhem: "8 Injured in Row Home Explosion in South Philadelphia," www.cbsnphilly.com. Fiasco: McPherson, Angie. "Slushy Sochi: Warm Weather Shows Challenges of Subtropical Snowmaking," www.nationalgeographic.com. Smithereens: Mead, Thomas. "Christchurch family restores stained glass windows shattered in earthquakes," www.newshub.co.nz. Pandemonium: "Soaked Glastonbury gets under way," www.bbc.com. Hazmat: Than, Ker. "Oil Spill Sullies Popular Tourist Beach in Thailand," www.nationalgeographic.com. Zany: Raymond, Tom. "Grock, Karl Adrien Wettach, inducted into the clown hall of fame in 1992," www.famousclowns.org. Rectify: Bartiromo, Michael. "Disney World cast member stops entire ride after guest tasks off mask, witness says," www.foxnews.com. Cadre: Morrison, Jim. "The True Story of the Monuments Men," www.smithsonianmag.com. Dumbfounded: Shapiro, Marc. Lorde. London, UK: Omnibus Press, 2014. Tomfoolery: Montgomery, L. M. (Lucy Maud). Anne of Green Gables. New York, NY: Bantam Books, 1976. Virtuoso: "100 Greatest Guitarists," www.rollingstone.com Satchel: Shakespeare, William. As You Like It. Edited by Barbara A. Mowat and Paul Werstine. (New York, NY: Simon & Schuster, 1997). Cantaloupe: Lewis, Norman. Word Power Made Easy. New York, NY: Anchor Books, 2014. Cheddar: McLean, Rachel E. "A Sharp Story: The Origin of Cheddar," www.culturecheesemag.com. Denim: Plautz, Jason. "10 Places and the Words They Inspired," www.mentalfloss.com. Frankfurter: Britannica, The Editors of Encyclopaedia. "Frankfurter," www.britannica.com. Satin: "Quanzhou," www.asiaculturaltravel.co.uk. Tuxedo: Green, Dennis. "We're entering a Golden Age of tuxedos – and these 8 photos show why," www.businessinsider.com. Magnify: "First magnifying glass," www.guinnessworldrecords.com. Provoke: Phillips, Kenneth M. "Dog Bite Law," www.dogbitelaw.com. Hubbub: "Falling Hare." Merrie Melodies, by Bob Clampett, Warner Brothers, 1943. Marvel: Lauer, Jonathon. "The History of Marvel Comics," www.thenerdd.com. Fussbudget: "The Browns and The Van Pelts: Siblings in Peanuts," www.schulzmuseum.org. Yelp: "Yelping in dogs can be a sign of pain or fear," www.canadianveterinarians.com. Spelunking: "Caving vs Spelunking – Is There a Difference?," www.outdoormotives.com. Delusion: Meares, Hadley. "The Delusion That Made Nobles Think Their Bodies Were Made of Glass," www.history.com. Woebegone: Mendoza Ph. D., Marilyn, A. "Professional Mourning: An Ancient Tradition," www.psychologytoday.com. Grapple: Nunley, Kim. "Grappling vs. Wrestling," www.sportsrec.com. Punctual: Walt Disney's Cinderella. Walt Disney Productions, 1950. Incorrigible:

Karetnick, Jen. "Service Dogs 101 – Everything You Need to Know," www.akc.com. Oodles: McLendon, Russell. "Surprising Ways Animals Stock Up for Winter," www.treehugger.com. Sabotage: Corera, Gordon. "How Britain pioneered cable-cutting in World War I," www.bbc.com. Dilapidated: "Bodie State Historic Park," www.parks.ca.gov. Tandem: Friend, Bonnie. "The Romantic History of Tandem Cycling," www.welovecycling.com Ailurophile: Howard, Harry. "The Cat Lady with the Lamp," www.dailymail.co.uk. Bibliophile: Camuccini, Vincenzo. "Ptolemy II Philadelphus Founds the Library of Alexandria," www.worldhistory.org. Cinephile: "The IMAX Difference," www.imaxmelbourne.com.au. Mycophile: Charles, Dan. "How a Sleepy Pennsylvania Town Grew Into America's Mushroom Capital," www.npr.org. Aplomb: Woo, Jeremy. "Top 100 NBA Players of 2021," www.sportsillustrated.com. Wanderlust: "About the TCC," www.travelerscenturyclub.org.Mastermind: Charnas, Dan. "The Rise and Fall of Hip-Hop's First Godmother: Sugar Hill Records' Sylvia Robinson," www.billboard.com. Docile: Shelley, Mary Wollstonecraft. Frankenstein, Or, The Modern Prometheus: the 1818 Text. New York, NY: Oxford University Press, 1998. Collaborate: Gagnon, Pauline. "The Forgotten Life of Einstein's First Wife," www.scientificamerican.com Nag: Jett & The Blackhearts, Joan. "Nag." I Love Rock 'n Roll. Boardwalk Records, 1981, LP. Bailiwick: "Meet the Hosts and Judges," www.pbs.org Glitch: Moses, Asher. "You are not here: Apple Maps app loses users," www.smh.com.au. Impromptu: Gallo, Carmine. "How Martin Luther King Improvised 'I Have A Dream,'" www.forbes.com. Squeamish: Kalter, Lindsay. "Nerves of steel, shaky stomachs," www.aamc.org. Quadrennial: Wood, Stephen. "5 Things You May Not Know About Leap Day," www.history.com. Cahoots: "Brink's Robbery," www.fbi.gov. Serendipity: McCafferty, Georgia. "Bought for $3 at yard sale, bowl sells for $2.2 million," www.cnn.com. Mishmash: "Mish Mash, Bulgarian omelet," www.balkanfoodrecipes.com. Panache: Williams, Keith. "When New Yorkers Fell for a Singer They Had Never Heard," www.nytimes.com. Liberate: Larosa, Brad. "How Stefani Germanotta Became Lady Gaga," www.abcnews.go.com. Hoopla: "What's New in Minneapolis: March Madness Edition," www.minneapolis.org. Madcap: It's A Mad, Mad, Mad, Mad World. Directed by Stanley Kramer, United Artists, 1963. Avuncular: Travers, P.L. Mary Poppins. Croydon, UK: HarperCollins, 2018. Jalopy: Pignat, Caroline. "Poppy's Jalopy," www.commonlit.org. Devour: Sesame Street, Sesame Workshop, 1969-2016. Rendezvous: "Space Rendezvous," www.nasa.gov. Captivating: Chewy Editorial. "Bronson the Cat's March Weight-Loss Update: One Cat Step Closer to His Goal," www.chewy.com. Concentric: "Rulebook," www.worldarchery.sport Peruse: Vergano, Dan. "Vatican Secret Archives holds tales fascinating... and not," www.usatoday.com. Blustery: "Fastest wind speed (recorded by an anemometer)," www.guinnessworldrecords.com Balmy: Zynda, Holly. "Weather Loses Meaning at the Equator," www.weatherunderground.com. Cold snap: Nace, Trevor. "'It's Almost Like Another Planet' – Coldest Temperature on Earth Recording in Antarctica," www.forbes.com. Scorcher: "Weather," www.nps.gov/deva Cyclone: Di Liberto, Tom.

"Tropical Cyclone Winston causes devastation in Fiji, a tropical paradise," www.climate.gov.Whiteout: Takahama, Elise. "Lost Mountain hiker starts to recover after rescue in whiteout conditions," www.seattletimes.com. Swanky: Donkey Kong Country 2: Diddy's Kong Quest. Nintendo, 1995. Zigzag: "Why doesn't lightning travel in a straight line?," www.cbcradio.ca. Humdinger: ATP Staff. "Djokovic Wins Eighth Australian Open Crown, Returns to No. 1," www.atptour.com. Orderly: Pollak, Michael. "The Story of Manhattan's Rectangular Street Grid," www.nytimes.com. Earworm: Kraemer, David J. M., et al. "Sound of silence activates auditory cortex," www.nature.com. Motley: Bad News Bears. Directed by Michael Ritchie, Paramount Pictures, 1976. Mojo: "Martial has got his mojo back," www.skysports.com. Turbulent: Thorpe, S.A. An Introduction to Ocean Turbulence. New York, NY: Cambridge University Press, 2007. Escalate: Carpenter, Megan. "How the Escalator Forever Changed Our Sense of Space," www.smithsonianmag.com. Sputter: "Internal Combustion Engine Basics," www.energy.gov. Egad: McCord, Carey P.M.D. "Medically Adrift; How to Be Profane Politely—Minced Oaths." Journal of Occupational and Environmental Medicine. Volume 65, Issue 5, May 2021 Brouhaha: Barron, James. "A Shell Is a Shell, No Matter Its Age," www.nytimes.com. Ludicrous: Pilcher, Rachel. "11 things you didn't know about ludacris," www.mtv.co.uk. Colossal: Caryl-Sue. "Big Blue," www.nationalgeographic.com Aghast: Longfellow, Henry Wadsworth. "The Wreck of Hesperus." Flummox: Forest, Heather. The Woman Who Flummoxed the Fairies. USA: August House, 1990. Trickle: Halvorson, Todd. "Astronaut with flooded helmet felt like goldfish in bowl," www.usatoday.com. Holluschick: "Facts about New Zealand fur seal," www.doc.govt.nz. Cignet: Britannica, The Editors of Encyclopaedia. "Swan," www.britannica.com. Elver: "American eel," www.fws.gov. Peachick: "Peacocks," www.nationalgeographic.com. Spat: Lu, Connie. "The relationship between oyster growing cycle and supply," www.pangeashellfish.com. Wiggler: Britannica, The Editors of Encyclopaedia. "Mosquito," www.britannica.com. Nevertheless: Reilly, Katie. "Why 'Nevertheless, She Persisted' Is the Theme for This Year's Women's History Month," www.time.com. Affable: "May 1 Was St. Tammany's Day," www.delawaretribe.org. Salinity: "Saline Water and Salinity," www.usgs.gov. Kibosh: Rogers, Jillian. "DOT: Paint over salmon murals on state roads," www.khns.org. Jolt: WECT. "Venomous fish at NC coast sends jolt of electricity through fisherman's arm," www.cbs17.com. Roundabout: "What is a roundabout?," www.wsdot.wa.gov Waver: Shepard, Julianne Escobedo. "Meet FKA Twigs, Music's New Fashion Darling," www.thecut.com. Bupkes: Allen, Petrer. "Couple who won and lost Lottery millions," www.dailymail.co.uk. Naught: "This Weekend's Boardmasters Festival 2019 Has Been Cancelled," www.kerrang.com. Diddly-Squat: Rumore, Kori. "How the rumor of 'Al Capone's Vaults' became a highly-rated, live TV special hosted by Geraldo Rivera 35 years ago today," www.chicagotribune.com. Zilch: Harrington, John et al. "A man sues himself? A docket of 25 of the weirdest, silliest and frivolous lawsuits," www.usatoday.com. Dillydally: "Don't Dilly Dally," www.racingpost.com. Swagger: Smith, Danyel. "The

Swagger Issue," Vibe, Jul. 2008. Flibbertigibbet: Greene, Harlan. "Gertrude Legendre – The High Life to Spy Life, And Back," www.charlestonmag.com. Antenna: "Extreme Space Facts," www.nasa.gov. Wordy: Kelly, John. "Oscars acceptance speeches have gotten longer over the decades," www. abc7chicago.com. Verisimilitude: Rowan, Jonathan Briche. "True to Life: A Study of Lifelikeness in Fiction through Proust, Austen, Nabokov, and Joyce," University of California, Berkeley, 2014. Gargoyle: "Darth Vader 'Gargoyle,'" www.cathedral.org. Axle: "Ten 'Fun and Exciting' Facts About Engineering," www. nspe.org.Raconteur: Andrew, Scottie. "How a 'Hamilton' song helped Amanda Gorman overcome a speech impediment," www.cnn.com. Retronym: "Penny-farthing History and Facts," www.bicyclehistory.net. Fossil: Moskvitch, Katia. "Ancient giant penguin unearthed in Peru," www.bbc.com.Relic: McSpadden, Kevin. "'Oscars of Chinese archaeology' reveals top 10 discoveries in China for 2020," www.scmp.com. Stratum: Harris, Stephen L., "Archaeology and Volcanism." Encyclopedia of Volcanoes, Cambridge, MA: Academic Press Books, 1999. Excavate: "Rising Star Expedition," www.nationalgeographic. org. Artifact: Learn, Joshua Rapp. "Before the Inca Ruled South America, the Tiwanaku Left Their Mark on the Andes," www. smithsonianmag.com. Coprolite: Prasad, Vandana et al. "Dinosaur Coprolites and the Early Evolution of Grasses and Grazers."Science Magazine, Nov. 2005 www.sciencemag.org. Beneficiary: Hannah, Felicity. "10 of the strangest wills of all time," www.theguardian.com. Uncouth: Crocket, Zachary. "The Worst Waiter in History," www.priceonomics.com. Procrastinator: Santella, Andrew. Soon: An Overdue History of Procrastination, from Leonardo and Darwin to You and Me. New York, NY: Dey Street Books, 2018. Incognito: Bushby, Helen. "From disguises to bad manners: How celebs avoid being pestered in public," www.bbc.com. Jubilee: "Showa Memorial Park," www.japan-guide.com.Fuddy-duddy: Apfel, Iris. Iris Apfel: Accidental Icon. New York, NY: Harper Design, 2018. Sangfroid: Ramaswamy, Chitra. "Britain's first female firefighter: 'The was no way I was going to be the weakest link,'" www.theguardian.com. Alias: Cronin, Brian. "TV Legends: Did Superman Actually Change in a Phone Booth on TV?" www.cbr. com. Castaway: Mackling, Robert. Castaway: The extraordinary survival of Narcisse Pelletier. Australia: Hachette Australia, 2019. Jetsam: Thomson, Andrew. "Artifacts Going Overboard," www.staugustinelighthouse.com. Salvage: "Ship Wrecks in the Cape Verdes," www.capeverdeinfo.org. Flotsam: Giaimo, Cara. "What's the Most Surprising Thing You've Ever Found Washed Up on the Beach?," www.atlasobscura.com. Capsize: Chen, Natasha. "New testimony reveals what happened before the Golden Ray capsized off the Georgia coast," www.cnn.com. Contend: "Mary Fields," www.nps.gov. Skyrocket: "Mentos and Diet Coke!," www.acs.org. Scoundrel: Darby, Mary. "In Ponzi We Trust," www. smithsonianmag.com. Defenestrate: "A Conversation with Mike Birbiglia," www.sleepfoundation.org. Befuddle: Boyle, Alan. "From Black Holes to Black History," www.nbcnews. com. Impetus: "Top 10 chemical reactions that you can repeat at home," www.melscience.com. Kerfuffle: Kellem, Betsy Golden. "When New York City Rioted Over Hamlet Being Too British," www.smithsonianmag.com. Bamboozle: Britannica, The Editors of Encyclopaedia. "Anansi," www.britannica.com. Domesticate: Rutledge, Kim et al. "Domestication," www. nationalgeographic.org. Exasperate: Paez, Danny. "How 'Rage Quit' Became the Most Relatable Gamer Emotion," www. inverse.com. Ruse: Aesop. Aesop's Fables. New York, NY: Oxford University Press, 2002. Omnibus: "Word Count and

Density," www.lotrproject.com. Pachyderm: "Top 10 Facts About Rhinos," www.wwforg.uk. Septillion: "Myth Buster: No Two Snowflakes Are Alike? Very Likely, But It's Hard to Prove," www.reconnectwithnature.org. Rubberneck: "Dashcam video shows multi-car crash in Beaumont caused by SpaceX launch," www.abc7.com. Doppelganger: Poe, Edgar Allen. The Works of Edgar Allan Poe, The Raven Edition, Volume 2. New York, NY: P.F. Collier and Son, 1903. Cyborg: Donahue, Michelle Z. "How a Color-Blind Artist Became the World's First Cyborg," www.nationalgeographic.com. Android: Hennessy, Michelle. "Makers of Sophia the robot plan mass rollout amid pandemic," www.reuters.com.Debug: Wall, Mike. "A Glitch Nearly Killed NASA's Curiosity Rover After 6 Months on Mars," www.space. com.Automation: "How will automation impact jobs?," www. pwc.co.uk. Actuator: "The history of automatic doors," www. theautomaticdoorco.com. Prototype: Newcomb, Alyssa. "Google's Newest Self-Driving Car Prototype: A Look Inside," www.abcnews.go.com. Troubadour: Britannica, The Editors of Encyclopaedia. "Woody Guthrie," www.britannica.com. Abhor: Petruzzello, Melissa. "Why Does Cilantro Taste Like Soap to Some People?" www.britannica.com. Recumbent: Kaza, Roger. "No. 2654 Bike Variations," www.uh.edu. Ecosystem: "5 of the World's Most Mind Blowing Ecosystems," www. goodnet.org. Squeegee: "2020 Speed Contest Rules," www. iwca.org. Harbinger: Andrews, Evan. "Eight Unusual Good Luck Charms," www.history.com. Curlicue: "Pig Info," www. pigspeace.org. Ponder: Thoreau, Henry David. Walden; or, Life in the Woods. New York, NY: Norton, 1992. Turbine: "Asbads (Windmill) of Iran," www.surfiran.com. Demolish: Kherdian, Robert. "The birth, life, and death of old Penn Station," www. ny.curbed.com. Honorary: Grundhauser, Eric. "Bosco the Dog Mayor," www.atlasobscura.com. Pompadour: Schneider, Martin. "Retro Rockabilly Gangs of Tokyo," www.dangerousminds. net. Ephemeral: "Flowering Times and Duration," www.tcss. wildapricot.org. Intransigent: Collinson, Alwyn. "How Bazalgette built London's first super-sewer," www.museumoflondon.org. uk. Lavation: Hernandez, Cathy. "Buc-ee's car wash in Katy gets Guinness record as world's longest," www.click2houston.com. Bugaboo: Buddle, Chris. "We Are We So Afraid Of Spiders?," www.independent.co.uk. Animator: Oppenheim, Maya. "Veteran Studio Ghibli animator spirited away at 77," www.independent. co.uk. Cosmetologist: "Madam C. J. Walker," www.history.com. Aviator: Maranzani, Barbara. "10 Things You May Not Know About the Roosevelts," www.history.com. Haberdasher: Scrivens, Louise. "Changing the flaws in London's laws," www. bbc.com. Entrepreneur: "City of Los Altos History Resources Inventory," www.losaltosca.gov. Volcanologist: Rowley, Dr. Keith. "How being a volcanologist helped me deal with pandemic," www.trinidadexpress.com. Heyday: Vance, Jeffrey. Chaplin: Genius Of The Cinema. New York, NY: Abrams Books, 2003. Mausoleum: "Mausoleum of the First Qin Emperor," www.unesco.org. Pizzazz: "Ten Incredible Elton John Performances," www.rollingstone.com. Nickelodeon: Britannica, The Editors of Encyclopaedia. "Nickelodeon," www.britannica. com. Hypothesis: Semple, Kirk. "Every Year, the Sky 'Rains Fish.' Explanations Vary.," www.nytimes.com. Marine: "How much of the ocean have we explored?," www.noaa.gov. Panacea: "The History of Antibiotics," www.microbiologysociety.org. Loggerheads: Wallisch, Pascal. "Two Years Later, We Finally Know Why People Saw 'The Dress' Differently," www.slate.com. Pulchritude: Wilde, Oscar. The Portrait of Dorian Gray. New York, NY: Penguin, 2003. Akimbo: "Swimming syndrome," www. vetbook.org. Durian: Ghosh, Prianka. "8 Things You Need To Know About Durian Fruit: The World's Smelliest Snack," www.

theculturetrip.com. Tamarind: Mertl-Millholen, Anne S. et al. "Tamarind tree seed dispersal by ring-tailed lemurs," www. pubmed.ncbi.nlm.nih.gov. Blackcurrant: Hermiston, Roger. All Behind You, Winston. London, UK: Aurum Press, 2016. Quandong: Grant, Amy. "Tips on Growing Quandong Fruit in Gardens," www.gardeningknowhow.com. Pitaya: "Dragon Fruit," www.agmrc.org. Opulent: Meares, Hadley. "How Versailles' Over-the-Top Opulence Drove the French to Revolt," www. history.com. Mulch: "5 Surprising Facts About Mulch," www. westminsterlawn.com. Zeppelin: Maksel, Rebecca. "Docking on the Empire State Building," www.airspacemag.com. Miniscule: Dell'Amore, Christine. "World's Smallest Frog Found—Fly-Size Beast Is Tiniest Vertebrate," www.nationalgeographic. org. Karaoke: Onishi, Norimitsu. "Sinatra Song Often Strikes Deadly Chord," www.nytimes.com. Sprocket: Raso, Michael. "Sprocket Hole Photography," www.filmphotographyproject. com. Disperse: "Dispersion: The Rainbow and Prisms," www. lumenlearning.com. Taboo: Blume, Judy. Are You There God? It's Me, Margaret. New York, NY: Atheneum Books for Young Readers, 2001. Accumulate: Cartwright, Mark. "Mansa Musa I," www.worldhistory.org. Killjoy: O'Neill, Therese. "5 of history's biggest killjoys," www.theweek.com. Monopoly: Thorpe, JR. "7 Hilarious Corrupt Politicians From History," www.bustle.com. Ambidextrous: "26 Celebrities Who Are Ambidextrous," www. ranker.com. Cicada: Bradford, Alina. "Facts About Cicadas," www.livescience.com. Botfly: Lidz, Frank. "I've Got Him Under My Skin," www.latimes.com. Katydid: Williams, Sarah C. P., "Why katydids sing in unison," www.sciencemag.com. Millipede: Morelle, Rebecca. "World's leggiest millipede put under microscope," www.bbc.com. Weevil: "Weevil: 9 General Types and How to Get Rid of Them," www.pestwiki.com. Mantis: Hadley, Debbie. "10 Fascinating Praying Mantis Facts," www. thoughtco.com. Aardvark: "Factsheet Aardvark," www.ypte. org.uk. Odoriferous: Daley, Jason. "Scientists Played Music to Cheese as It Aged. Hip-Hop Produced the Funkiest Flavor," www.smithsonianmag.com. Igloo: Holihan, Rich et al. "How Warm is an Igloo?" Cornell University, 2003. Abacus: "Largest abacus," www.guinnessworldrecords.com. Camouflage: Jones, Benji. "Chameleons' Craziest Color Changes Aren't for Camouflage," www.nationalgeographic.org. Odyssey: Long, Tony. "Nov. 14, 1889: Around the World in Only 72 Days," www.wired.com. Fortnight: Ott, Michael. "Pope Urban VII." The Catholic Encyclopedia. New York, NY: Robert Appleton Company, 1912. Chitchat: Tolin, Lisa. "Master Small Talk: Why You Need Chit-Chat in Your Life," www.nbcnews.com. Comeuppance: Greene, Nick. "Elvis Presley's Bizarre Album of Stage Banter," www.mentalfloss.com. Pareidolia: McLendon, Russell. "14 Eerie 'Faces' of Pareidolia from Nature," www. treehugger.com. Asteroid: "Hayabusa Spacecraft Returns Asteroid Artifacts From Space," www.nasa.gov. Gibbous: "Gibbous Moon," www.astronomy.swin.edu.au. Extraterrestrial: Loeb, Avi. Extraterrestrial: The First Sign of Intelligent Life Beyond Earth. New York, NY: Houghton Mifflin Harcourt, 2021. Lunar: Osborne, Hannah. "Harrison Schmitt, the Last Man to Walk on the Moon, Was Allergic to Moon Dust—Warns Others May Be Too," www.newsweek.com. Nebula: "Helix Nebula – Unraveling at the Seams," www.nasa.gov. Supernova: "Supernovae," www.nationalgeographic.com. Deciduous: "8 interesting facts about autumn," www.metoffice.gov.uk. Phenomenon: Gamillo, Elizabeth. "Yosemite's 'Firefall' Natural Wonder Illuminates El Capitan Through the End of February," www.smithsonianmag.com. Temerity: Smith, Harrison. "Kitty O'Neil, deaf daredevil who became 'world's fastest woman,' dies at 72," www.washingtonpost.com. Cuckoo: Stamp,

Jimmy. "The Past, Present, and Future of the Cuckoo Clock," www.smithsonianmag.com. Ostentatious: McMah, Lauren. "Inside the insanely decadent life of the Sultan of Brunei," www.news.com.au. Trajectory: Slotnik, Daniel E. "No Matter the Game, Babe Didrikson Zaharias Played to Win," www.nytimes.com. Unique: Jeddy, Nadeem et all. "Tongue prints in biometric authentication: A pilot study." Journal of Oral and Maxillofacial Pathology, Jan-Apr. 2017. Regenerate: "Can You Live Without Your Liver?," www.upmc.com. Cornucopia: Grundhauser, Eric. "From Zeus to Williams-Sonoma: The History of the Cornucopia," www.atlasobscura.com. Quid pro quo: "Chimpanzee Habitat," www.conservenature.org. Juggernaut: Britannica, The Editors of Encyclopaedia. "Great hurricane of 1780," www.britannica.com. Agenda: Andrews, Evan. "8 Historical Figures with Unusual Work Habits," www.history.com. Crochet: Salomone, Andrew. "Yarn-Bombing Artist Sets Out to Crochet Across The USA," www.vice.com. Adjacent: Daley, Jason. "Archaeologists Uncover an Ancient Roman Game Board at Hadrian's Wall," www.smithsonianmag.com. Cerulean: Larson, Anna G. et al. "Pantone's Colors of the Year represent a changing world," www.duluthnewstribune.com. Puce: Challamel, Augustin. The History of Fashion In France: Or The Dress Of Women From The Gallo-Roman Period To The Present Time. Washington, D.C.: Westphalia Press, 2018. Flaxen: Dickens, Charles. David Copperfield. New York, NY: Modern Library, 2000. Cyan: "CMYK," www.techterms.com. Periwinkle: Braid, Fara. "Lapis Lazuli Symbolism," www.gemsociety.org. Chartreuse: Kelleher, Katy. "Chartreuse, the Color of Elixirs, Flappers, and Alternate Realities," www.theparisreview.org. Dilute: Little, Becky. "When London Faced a Pandemic – And a Devastating Fire," www.history.com. Scuttlebutt: Linder, Douglas. "The Witchcraft Trials in Salem: A Commentary," www.umkc.edu. Aboveboard: Niiler, Eric. "Soccer Is Getting Slower and More Fair—and That's a Problem," www.wired.com. Demure: Post, Emily. Emily Post's Etiquette, 18th edition. New York: HarperCollins Publishers, 2004. Inflation: Jones, Paul Anthony. "Hyperinflation Gone Mad: When German Children Made Kites From Money," www.mentalfloss.com. Perspire: Phillips, Quinn. "When It Comes to Sweat, What's Considered Normal?" www.everydayhealth.com. Predict: Breitman, Daniela. "Today In Science: Discovery Of Neptune," www.earthsky.org. Juxtapose: Zielinski, Sarah. "Comparing Apples and Oranges," www.smithsonianmag.com. Rustic: "Rustic Architecture: 1916 – 1942," www.nps.gov. Spurn: Knorovsky, Katie. "Travel through time with 21 women explorers who changed the world," www.nationalgeographic.com. Kerplunk: "Miami Pays Damages For Falling Coconut." Ocala Star-Banner, Oct. 4, 1956. Conclave: Glod, Maria. "Odd Fellows Have Skeletons in Their Closets – and Their Walls and Attics," www.latimes.com. Ignite: "How Car Engines Work: Lesson for Kids," www.study.com. Acupuncture: "Acupuncture," www.mayoclinic.com. Vice versa: Chernow, Ron. Alexander Hamilton. New York, NY: Penguin Group, 2004. Slapstick: In the Sweet Pie and Pie. Directed by Jules White, Columbia Pictures, 1941. Schmooze: Avery, Dan. "This Artist Faked Being a Billionaire to Photograph New York City's Best Views," www.architecturaldigest.com. Alter: Dixon, Emily. "Here's How Princess Beatrice Altered One of the Queen's Favorite Dresses for Her Wedding," www.marieclaire.com. Musical Words: "Dynamics," www.phoenixsymphony.org. Superfluous: "Great Pacific Garbage Patch," www.nationalgeographic.org. Mangle: "Barnett Newman," www.stedelijk.nl. Scholar: "Science and technology in Medieval Islam," www.mhs.ox.ac.uk. Whodunit: "10 Facts About Agatha Christie Fans Should Know," www.southernliving.com. Topsy-turvy: Hirst, K. Kris. "The Dust Veil Environmental Disaster of AD 536," www.thoughtco.com. Derive: Alfaro, Danilo. "What Are Marshmallows Made Of?" www.thespruceeats.com. Pugnacious: Cohen, Patricia. "Reason Seen More as Weapon Than Path to Truth," www.nytimes.com. Noodge: Hoovley, Evan. "6 Beloved Scientists Who Were Actually Total Jerks," www.syfy.com. Rickety: "Louvre to exhibit Balintore shed door marble bust," www.bbc.com. Edible: Gelling, Natasha. "The Science Behind Honey's Eternal Shelf Life," www.smithsonianmag.com. Malaise: Kaulessar, Ricardo. "Can you actually get sick from the weather changing?" www.northjersey.com. Apparition: Young, Nick. "Who Exactly Are The Ghosts Of London?" www.londonist.com. Eerie: Travers, Penny. "National Film and Sound Archive one of Australia's 'most haunted buildings,'" www.abc.net.au. Macabre: Nuwer, Rachel. "'Vampire Grave' in Bulgaria Holds a Skeleton With a Stake Through Its Heart," www.smithsonianmag.com. Hobgoblin: "The Meaning of Bwbach Explained," www.bluestonewales.com. Gruesome: Shum, Sharon. "Krasue is the Girl with Serious Detachment Issues," www.vice.com. Phantasm: Mapes, Diane. "Have you seen a ghost? There may be a medical reason," www.today.com. Establish: Pinsker, Joe. "Japan's Oldest Businesses Have Survived for More Than 1,000 Years," www.theatlantic.com. Boffo: Zimmer, Ben. "'Boffo': Donald Trump's Show-Biz Slang for Success, Applied to Politics," www.wsj.com. Charisma: "The Bronz Fonz," www.visitmilwaukee.org. Buoyant: Colby, Terri. "Living it up in the Dead Sea," www.chicagotribune.com. Aloof: "Emily Dickinson," www.biography.com. Erratic: Barrett, Judi. Cloudy With a Chance of Meatballs. New York, NY: Aladdin Paperbacks, 1982. Medicinal: Smith, Andrew F. "Tomato Pills Will Cure All Your Ills." Pharmacy in History, 1991. Inherit: Bubenik, George A. "Why do humans get 'goosebumps' when they are cold, or under other circumstances?," www.scientificamerican.com. Yo: Dalzell, Tom. Flappers 2 Rappers: American Youth Slang. Springfield, MA: Merriam-Webster, Inc., 1996. Landlocked: Dempsey, Caitlin. "Landlocked Countries," www.geographyrealm.com. Pyretic: Klibanoff, Eleanor. "You Might Be Surprised When You Take Your Temperature," www.npr.org. Pruritus: "Itchy skin (pruritus)," www.mayoclinic.org. Whippersnapper: "Greta Thunberg: Who is she and what does she want?" www.bbc.com. Grevillea: "Seed Notes for Western Australia," www.dpaw.wa.gov.au. Chrysanthemum: "History of the Chrysanthemum," www.mums.org. Foxglove: "The incredible tale of the foxglove, from curing to disease to inspiring Van Gogh's most striking paintings," www.countrylife.co.uk. Edelweiss: The Sound of Music. Directed by Robert Wise, 20th Century Fox, 1965. Dogwood: Bartons, Siobhan. "All About The Flowering Dogwood," www.thetreecenter.com. Thistle: "About Scotland's National Flowers," www.visitscotland.com. Widget: Lowensohn, Josh. "A brief history of widgets," www.theverge.com. Thermal: Palermo, Elizabeth. "Eiffle Tower: Information & Facts," www.livescience.com. Harsh: Hiskey, Daven. "Camels Have Three Eyelids," www.todayifoundout.com. Caustic: "Sodium Hydroxide," www.chemicalsafetyfacts.org. Moniker: Solomon, Deborah. "Questions for Whoopi Goldberg: Making Nice," www.nytimes.com. Concoction: Pope, Shelby. "How An 11-Year-Old Boy Invented The Popsicle," www.npr.org. Pivotal: Weintraub, Karen. "20 Years After Dolly the Sheep Led the Way—Where Is Cloning Now?," www.scientificamerican.com. Parapet: "The Origin of The Parapet," www.iroofing.org. Kiosk: Goldstein, Danielle. "Meet the man (and his mum) running London's oldest newstand: Haines of Sloane Square," www.timeout.com. Hobnob: "Le Drian case: Fraudsters who wore mask of French minister jailed," www.bbc.com. Erupt: "Pompeii: Ancient 'fast food' counter to open to the public," www.bbc.com. Vamoose: "Historic Flood – 1950," www.gov.mb.ca. Descendant: Borkhataria, Cecile. "Planet of the Rats," www.dailymail.co.uk. Swarm: GrrlScientist. "Drone Light Shows 'Way Cooler' Than Fireworks," www.forbes.com. Abominable: Barksdale, Nate. "8 Things You May Not Know About Henry VIII," www.history.com. Satire: Geisler, Michael E. National Symbols, Fractured Identities: Contesting the National Narrative. Lebanon, NH: University Press of New England, 2005. Venture: "Sacagawea," www.biography.com. Anorak: "Anorak," www.macmillandictionaryblog.com. Pince-nez: "Hindsight Is 20/20: The Prince-Nez," www.2020mag.com. Balaclava: Hartston, William. "Top 10 facts about the Crimean War," www.express.co.uk.Cummerbund: Britannica, The Editors of Encyclopaedia. "Cummerbund," www.britannica.com. Knickerbockers: Newman, Alex. Fashion A to Z: An Illustrated Dictionary. London, UK: Laurence King Publishing Ltd., 2012. Galoshes: Peeples, Lynne. "The Origin of Rubber Boots," www.scientificamerican.com. Physically: Back to the Future. Directed by Robert Zemeckis, Universal Pictures, 1985. Physically: "Commonwealth Coat of Arms," www.pmc.gov.au. Whirlybird: Mangan, Gregg. On This Day in Connecticut History. Charleston, SC: History Press, 2015 Aft: "15 Basic Boat Terms," www.wavesboatclub.com. Naan: Dash, Madhulika. "Food Story: How Naan and Kulcha became India's much-loved breads," www.indianexpress.com. Challah: "The Significance of Challah," www.modernistbread.com. Fry bread: Miller, Jen. "Frybread," www.smithsonianmag.com. Injera: Liu, Karon. "Ethiopian injera a tradition that spans thousands of years," www.thestar.com. Lavash: Leahy, Kate. "On the Lavash Trail in Armenia," www.smithsonianmag.com. Focaccia: Baldwin, Eleonora. "A brief history of focaccia," www.theamericanmag.com. Tradition: "Songkran: Thailand celebrates Buddhist new year with water fights," www.bbc.com. Caravan: "Caravanserai," www.nationalgeographic.org. Jocular: "Moms Mabley," www.biography.com.Knickknack: "Knickknack Peddler, 13th-15th century," www.metmuseum.org. Exorbitant: Desai, Yash. "La Collection de Bijoux : The most expensive Dog Diamonds," www.businessinsider.com. Fluorescent: Signorelli, Laura. "Ten interesting facts about sharks," www.sea.museum. Ballistics: Gill, Victoria. "Oldest evidence of arrows found," www.bbc.com. Penultimate: "Live: Candlestick Park, San Francisco: The Beatles' final concert," www.beatlesbible.com. Ebullient: Gillespie, Dizzy. The Ebullient Mr. Gillespie, Verve, 1959.

Illustrations

Josy Bloggs
Pgs 8, 20, 40, 43, 46, 48, 51–52, 53, 55, 60–61, 67, 68, 70–71, 80–81, 84, 100, 107, 111, 113, 125, 127, 128, 130–31, 132, 138, 161, 165, 169, 176–77, 180, 182–83, 186–87, 190, 193, 194, 200, 203, 208–9, 213, 216, 219, 220, 223, 224, 229, 243, 244, 246, 251, 253, 254, 257, 258, 261, 267, 268, 272–73, 275, 289, 290–91, 299, 313, 336–37, 341, 343, 348–49

Emily Cox
Pgs 6, 13, 36, 42, 44, 46–47, 54, 58–59, 66, 74, 79, 87, 90–91, 96, 98, 103, 104–5, 106, 133, 137, 142, 143, 144, 150, 155, 156, 159, 160, 166, 171, 172, 175, 188, 191, 192, 195, 196–97, 198–99, 201, 202, 211, 214–15, 217, 218, 221, 222, 226–27, 228, 236, 240, 242, 245, 247, 252, 266, 279, 284, 286–87, 295, 302, 306–7, 310, 326, 328, 330–31

James Gibbs
Pgs 9, 14–15, 16–17, 18, 21, 22, 27, 28, 35, 39, 49, 50, 56, 65, 76–77, 83, 88–89, 95, 99, 101, 108, 110, 117, 118–19, 129, 146–47, 153, 162–163, 164, 167, 174, 189, 210, 237, 239, 248–49, 262–63, 270, 274, 276–77, 278, 282, 285, 288, 294, 297, 300–1, 305, 308, 311, 312, 314–15, 316–17, 319, 324, 327, 329, 332, 334–35, 340, 342, 344–45

Liz Kay
Pgs 7, 10–11, 12, 19, 23, 24–25, 26, 29, 30–31, 34, 37, 38, 41, 57, 64, 69, 72–73, 75, 78, 82, 85, 86, 94, 97, 102, 109, 112, 114–15, 116, 122–123, 124, 126, 134–35, 136, 139, 140–41, 145, 151, 152, 154, 157, 158, 168, 170, 173, 181, 184–85, 204–5, 212, 225, 230–31, 232–33, 238, 241, 250, 255, 256, 259, 260, 269, 271, 280–81, 283, 296, 298, 303, 304, 309, 318, 320–21, 325, 333, 338, 339, 346–47